Grammarsaurus

THE ULTIMATE GUIDE

TO TEACHING NON-FICTION WRITING, SPELLING, PUNCTUATION AND GRAMMAR

MITCH HUDSON
ANNA RICHARDS

BLOOMSBURY EDUCATION
LONDON OXFORD NEW YORK NEW DELHI SYDNEY

BLOOMSBURY EDUCATION
Bloomsbury Publishing Plc
50 Bedford Square, London, WC1B 3DP, UK
29 Earlsfort Terrace, Dublin 2, Ireland

BLOOMSBURY, BLOOMSBURY EDUCATION and the Diana logo are trademarks of Bloomsbury Publishing Plc
First published in Great Britain, 2021, by Bloomsbury Publishing Plc
Text copyright © Mitch Hudson and Anna Richards, 2021
Illustrations copyright © Shutterstock

Material from Department for Education documents used in this publication is approved under an Open Government licence: www.nationalarchives.gov.uk/doc/open-government-licence/version/3

Mitch Hudson and Anna Richards have asserted their right under the Copyright, Designs and Patents Act, 1988, to be identified as Authors of this work

Bloomsbury Publishing Plc does not have any control over, or responsibility for, any third-party websites referred to or in this book. All internet addresses given in this book were correct at the time of going to press. The author and publisher regret any inconvenience caused if addresses have changed or sites have ceased to exist, but can accept no responsibility for any such changes

All rights reserved. This book may be photocopied, for use in the educational establishment for which it was purchased, but may not be reproduced in any other form or by any other means – graphic, electronic, or mechanical, including photocopying, recording, taping or information storage or retrieval systems – without prior permission in writing of the publishers

A catalogue record for this book is available from the British Library

ISBN: PB 978-1-4729-8121-9; ePDF 978-1-4729-8123-3

2 4 6 8 10 9 7 5 3 1

Cover design by James Fraser
Text design by Jeni Child

Printed and bound in the UK by CPI Group Ltd, Croydon CR0 4YY

To find out more about our authors and books visit www.bloomsbury.com and sign up for our newsletters

Dedications

For the three teachers who ignited my passion for the English language – Miss Capewell, Mrs Holland and Miss Porter – and for my parents, Janice and Ian, who always taught me to work the very hardest for my dreams.

Mitch

For my parents who taught me that education is the most important and powerful weapon in life; to my husband, Dan, and darling daughter, Rosie, for being my world; and to my co-author, Mitch, who made this dream a reality.

Anna

Contents

Grammarsaurus KS1© Mitch Hudson and Anna Richards 2021

Introduction

As teachers, we often searched for texts to use in the classroom and struggled to find ones that were of a high quality and appropriate for the children we were teaching: either they didn't have the right grammar coverage, the context wasn't appropriate, or the children had already studied the text in a different year group! This wasn't just our own experience, as we also witnessed this when working with other teachers in our school and in other school settings in our roles as SLEs and moderators.

We felt that teachers would benefit from a book which would allow them to easily access high-quality texts which were both age-appropriate and contained the relevant writing, grammar, spelling and punctuation from the National Curriculum and the teacher assessment frameworks. We strongly believe that these skills should be taught in context, rather than in standalone grammar or punctuation lessons.

Equally, we knew that grammar could be fun! We wanted to make sure that the texts we wrote were engaging for children of all ages and linked to the topics featured in the National Curriculum.

The Grammarsaurus website has always had a strong community spirit, with our followers helping to make key decisions such as the design of the logo, the colour scheme for the website, and even the title of the Grammarsaurus books. Therefore, it seemed right that our followers decided the topics the texts would focus on via an online poll.

The texts cover a range of contexts and topics: factual and imaginative, historical and current. Whilst the texts were written for particular year groups, you can use them for the other year groups too. They can be adapted to suit different year groups or used as inspiration to write your own.

We understand the confusion and uncertainty that sometimes surrounds 'working at a greater depth' as mentioned in the teacher assessment frameworks at the end of Key Stages 1 and 2. This is why we have included two texts for Year 2: one at the 'expected standard' and one at 'greater depth'.

We hope this book will support you when deciding what skills to teach and when. We ourselves use our text-specific overviews and model texts when planning: they are invaluable to us, and we hope they will become invaluable to you, too! The overviews will help you to decide when to teach different skills and the model texts will show how these skills can be used in different contexts. Whether you use the model texts to support your own knowledge or share them with your pupils to expose them to high-quality texts, we are sure they will be a great support.

Grammarsaurus KS1© Mitch Hudson and Anna Richards 2021

How to use this book

Each chapter of this book focuses on a different non-fiction text type: instructional texts, explanation texts, non-chronological reports, recounts (diary), recounts (newspaper) and persuasive texts. Each chapter contains the following:

Teaching tips

These are ideas that we have found to be effective in teaching children to write different styles of text and tackling the common difficulties that tend to crop up during teaching.

Text-specific overviews

These overviews are separated into the following areas: text-specific features (e.g. a headline is a feature of a newspaper article) and the grammar, punctuation and spelling opportunities that you may expect to cover for that text type.

Text-specific features

These could be considered to be the 'building blocks' for writing different text types. For example, persuasive texts will include features like flattery and emotive language, whereas a non-chronological report will contain subheadings and factual statements.

Grammar, punctuation and spelling lists

These are some key grammar, spelling and punctuation opportunities that come up in the model texts. Under many of the points are example words, phrases or sentences.

Checklists

Each overview page ends with a checklist which teachers and children can use alongside the model texts. These can be used as a handy guide to aid planning and to support children's writing. The checklists highlight the features contained in the model texts and can be used for self, peer or teacher assessment.

These checklists are guides and not exhaustive lists. The model texts include many other grammar, spelling and punctuation opportunities, which are not listed in the checklists, and these can be taught where you think it is appropriate.

Model texts

Each model text has been written to meet the 'expected standard' or 'greater depth standard' for Year 1 or Year 2 pupils. To make the features of the model text clear to you, we have included two versions:

1. Unannotated: these can be photocopied for pupils or displayed on a whiteboard or projector.
2. Annotated: the text-specific features and grammar, punctuation and spelling opportunities are all clearly detailed in this version.

You can use the model texts in a variety of ways. You can read them as examples of the expected standards for each year group and explore the different features present in each text. You can share the texts with your pupils, perhaps inviting them to annotate the texts themselves. You could even share the annotated texts with children to help them evaluate the writing.

Topic coverage

Grammarsaurus Key Stage 1 and its companion book for Key Stage 2 cover a wide range of topics, including history, geography and science. Here is an overview of the topic coverage for both books. This book is for Years 1 and 2 only.

	Instructional texts	Explanation texts	Non-chronological reports	Recounts: diary entries	Recounts: newspaper articles	Persuasive texts
Year 1	How to prepare for a teddy bears' picnic	How is bread made?	Arctic animals	School trip to the seaside	***Not appropriate for Year 1 level***	Jack's magic beans
Year 2	How to find buried treasure	How do plants grow?	Marine mammals	A pirate's life	London's Burning!	T-Rex in town
Year 2 greater depth	How to build a castle	How do food chains work?	Kings and queens	Antarctic adventures	Gunpowder, Treason and Capture!	Adopt a wild animal!
Year 3	How to make a wizard's spell	How do shadow puppets work?	Roman soldiers	Queen Boudicca	Man Walks on the Moon!	Marvellous Mike's travelling circus
Year 4	How to survive an earthquake	How does the water cycle work?	The Titanic	Viking raider	Peril in Pompeii!	Ascend the astral throne!
Year 5	How to prepare for an intergalactic mission	How do volcanoes erupt?	Ancient Greek myths: the cyclops	The discovery of Tutankhamun's tomb	Marathon Man Brings News of Victory!	Join the Stellar Dome Community today!
Year 6	How to survive a zombie attack	How does blood circulate around the body?	The ancient Maya	Darwin's diary: The Galápagos Islands	Normandy Invaded!	Join the Women's Land Army
Year 6 greater depth	How to survive on a desert island	How does the internet work?	The Shang Dynasty	The mystery of the Mary Celeste	Heir to the Montagues Gatecrashes Ball	Visit the Great Exhibition

Grammarsaurus KS1© Mitch Hudson and Anna Richards 2021

Useful words for Key Stage 1

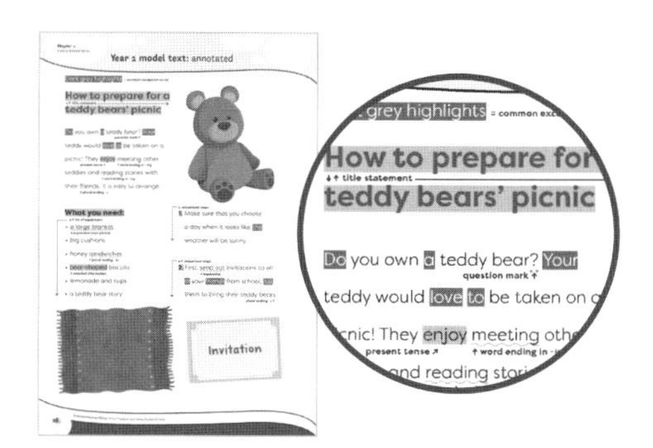

The National Curriculum in England lists 'common exception words' that are statutory for pupils to learn in Key Stage 1. We have included these below. Whenever these words appear in the model texts, we have highlighted them, so you can quickly see which words are key spellings for children to learn.

Year 1 common exception words

a	one
are	our
ask	pull
be	push
by	put
come	said
do	says
friend	school
full	she
go	so
has	some
he	the
here	there
his	they
house	to
I	today
is	was
love	we
me	were
my	where
no	you
of	your
once	

Year 2 common exception words

after	fast	pass
again	father	past
any	find	path
bath	floor	people
beautiful	gold	plant
because	grass	poor
behind	great	pretty
both	half	prove
break	hold	should
busy	hour	steak
child	improve	sugar
children	kind	sure
Christmas	last	told
class	many	water
climb	mind	who
clothes	money	whole
cold	most	wild
could	move	would
door	Mr	
even	Mrs	
every	old	
everybody	only	
eye	parents	

Instructional texts

The purpose of an instructional text is to help the reader learn something by providing a step-by-step guide.

Tips for teaching children to write instructional texts

- Younger children and less confident writers can find it easier to write about things they have experienced. Consider inviting them to write about a simple recipe like making a sandwich or allowing the children to create something crafty, which they can then write about.

- Consider different ways children could plan their writing. Remind the children about the different sections of an instructional text, for example, 'introduction', 'equipment list' and 'method'. Invite children to plan and write each section separately in boxes on a page to make the process easier.

- To support children to write in chronological order, choose a topic and provide children with the steps involved on separate pieces of card. Ask children to place the steps in the correct order.

- To scaffold less confident writers, take photographs of the children as they complete a task and display them so that they have a visual reminder of what they did at each step, to use while they write.

- Discuss how the use of adverbials of time can make it easier to write chronological steps. Encourage children to use more detailed adverbials in their own writing. For example, instead of writing '**After that**, prepare the icing', children might write something more detailed such as '**After the cake has been placed in the oven**, prepare the icing'.

- Teach a range of adverbials of time, including adverbial clauses, to add variety when children are writing a method. Otherwise, they may overuse 'next' and 'then'.

  - **Following that**
  - **Once _____ has been completed**
  - **When you have finished _____**
  - **After _____ minutes**
  - **Once the _____ starts to _____**

- Create an anchor chart (a visual prompt that provides children with information on a theme) with a range of examples of quantifiers to encourage the children to write expanded noun phrases for description and specification.

  - **several**
  - **a slither of**
  - **a selection of**
  - **three spoonfuls of**
  - **two handfuls of**
  - **a large variety of**

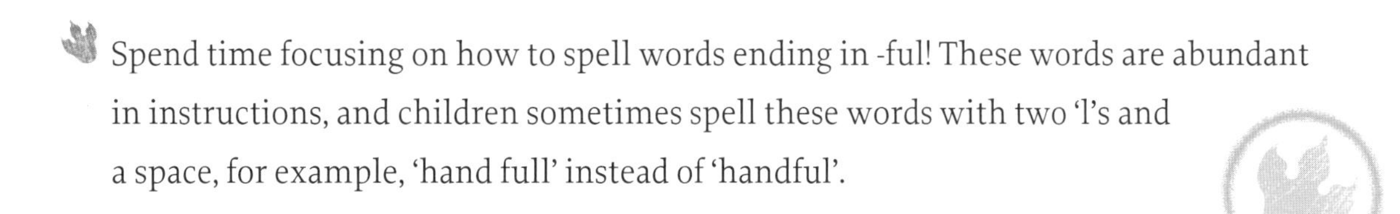

- Spend time focusing on how to spell words ending in -ful! These words are abundant in instructions, and children sometimes spell these words with two 'l's and a space, for example, 'hand full' instead of 'handful'.

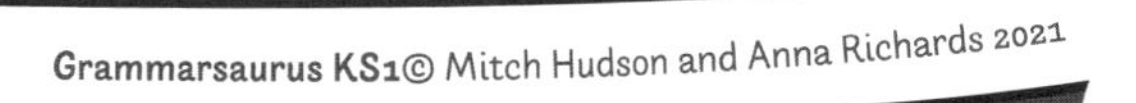

Grammarsaurus KS1© Mitch Hudson and Anna Richards 2021

Year 1 overview

Use this overview and the checklist alongside the Year 1 model text (pages 14 – 17).

Specific features for this text type

Feature	Example
• A title statement explaining what is to be achieved	*How to make a jam sandwich.*
• A list of equipment or materials	*You will need the following items...*
• Sequenced, chronological steps	*First, second, third...* *Next, then, after that...*
• Diagrams or illustrations	
• Present tense	*These steps explain how to make a perfect jam sandwich!*
• Commands (use imperative verbs)	*Slice the bread.*
• Detailed information – prepositions, determiners and precise vocabulary	*Place one piece of bread...* *You will need two slices of bread.*

The following lists should be used as a tool to help teachers plan where to cover explicit grammar, punctuation and spelling objectives from the National Curriculum Programmes of Study.

Grammar

Feature	Example
• Coordinating conjunctions – link ideas with 'and'	*Place the bread on the work surface and spread the butter...*
• Expanded noun phrases – add detail to nouns using prepositions such as 'of', 'under', 'around', 'next to' and 'above'	*the crust of the bread*
• Positional language	*on the plate*

Punctuation

Feature	Example
• Question marks	*Do you love the taste of scrumptious strawberry jam?*

Spelling

- Year 1 'common exception words' from the National Curriculum: see page 9 of this book for a list of these. These common exception words are highlighted in the Year 1 model text.

• Plurals of nouns ending in -s or -es	*jars, sandwiches*
• Verbs ending in -ing	*mixing, adding, spreading*

Checklist

Use this checklist with the Year 1 model text. See page 7 for more information.

Title statement	
List of equipment or materials	
Sequenced, chronological steps	
Diagrams or illustrations	
Present tense	
Commands	
Detailed information	
Grammar: Coordinating conjunctions	
Grammar: Expanded noun phrases	
Grammar: Positional language	
Punctuation: Question marks	
Spelling: Year 1 common exception words	
Spelling: Plurals of nouns ending in -s or -es	
Spelling: Verbs ending in -ing	

Grammarsaurus KS1© Mitch Hudson and Anna Richards 2021

Year 1 model text

How to prepare for a teddy bears' picnic

Do you own a teddy bear? Your teddy would love to be taken on a picnic! They enjoy meeting other teddies and reading stories with their friends. It is easy to arrange.

You will need these things:

- a large blanket
- big cushions
- honey sandwiches
- bear-shaped biscuits
- lemonade and cups
- a teddy bear story.

1. Make sure that you choose a day when it looks like the weather will be sunny.

2. First, send out invitations to all of your friends from school. Ask them to bring their teddy bears.

Grammarsaurus KS1© Mitch Hudson and Anna Richards 2021

3. On the day of the picnic, find a space in the woods or the park, under the trees.

4. Then, put the blanket on the ground and the big cushions around the edge.

5. Next, share the food with everyone there.

6. Finally, read everyone the teddy bear story before they pack up to go home.

Warning!

Teddies can get very tired and they like to go to bed early. Make sure that you do not stay at the park or woods too late. Plan to have the picnic during the afternoon.

Year 1 model text: annotated

Dark grey highlights = common exception words

How to prepare for a teddy bears' picnic

↓↑ title statement

Do you own a teddy bear? Your teddy would love to be taken on a picnic! They enjoy meeting other teddies and reading stories with their friends. It is easy to arrange.

question mark ↑ · present tense ↗ · ↑ word ending in -ing · ↑ word ending in -ing · ↑ plural ending -s

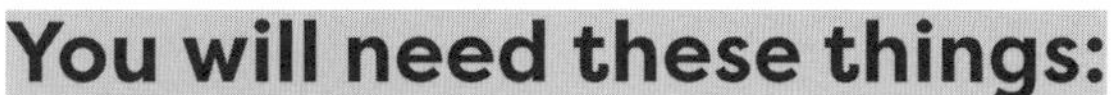

You will need these things:

↓↑ list of equipment

- a large blanket
  ↑ expanded noun phrase
- big cushions
- honey sandwiches
  ↑ plural ending -es
- bear-shaped biscuits
  ↑ detailed information
- lemonade and cups
- a teddy bear story.

↓ sequenced steps

1. Make sure that you choose a day when it looks like the weather will be sunny.

↓↑ sequenced steps

2. First, send out invitations to all of your friends from school. Ask them to bring their teddy bears.
   ↑ command · plural ending -s ↑

Grammarsaurus KS1© Mitch Hudson and Anna Richards 2021

↓↑ sequenced steps
3. On the day of the picnic, find a
↑ expanded noun phrase
space in the woods or the park, under the trees.
↑ positional language

↓↑ sequenced steps
4. Then, put the blanket on the ground and the big cushions around the edge.
↑ coordinating conjunction

↓↑ sequenced steps
5. Next, share the food with everyone there.

↓↑ sequenced steps
6. Finally, read everyone the
expanded noun phrase ↗
teddy bear story before they
↖ expanded noun phrase
pack up to go home.

Warning!

Teddies can get very tired and they like to go to
↑ coordinating conjunction
bed early. Make sure that you do not stay at the
↑ command
park or woods too late. Plan to have the picnic
↑ command
during the afternoon.

Year 2 overview

Use this overview and the checklist alongside the Year 2 model texts (pages 20 – 27).

Specific features for this text type

• A title statement explaining what is to be achieved	*How to build a sandcastle.*
• A list of equipment or materials	*Equipment list:*
• Sequenced, chronological steps	*First, second, third...* *Then, after that, following that...*
• Diagrams or illustrations	
• Present tense	*The sand must be wet.*
• Commands (use imperative verbs)	*Use a bucket.* *Collect the water.*
• Detailed information – use prepositions, determiners and precise vocabulary	*Smooth the top of the castle.* *Build four walls around the castle.*

The following lists should be used as a tool to help teachers plan where to cover explicit grammar, punctuation and spelling objectives from the National Curriculum Programmes of Study.

Grammar

• Coordinating conjunctions – link ideas with 'and', 'or' or 'but'	*Use a round bucket or a square one.*
• Subordinating conjunctions – expand upon independent clauses using 'if' and 'when'	*When the foundation has been built...*
• Expanded noun phrases – add detail to nouns using prepositions such as 'of' or 'under'	*the walls of the castle*
• Direct address to the reader using the second person pronoun 'you'	*You must follow these instructions carefully.*
• Adverbials of place	*on top of the keep* *surrounding the sandcastle*

Grammarsaurus KS1© Mitch Hudson and Anna Richards 2021

Punctuation

• Question marks	***Are you enjoying the sand between your toes?***
• Commas for lists	***bucket, spade and water***
• Apostrophes for possession (GDS)	***the castle's keep***
• Apostrophes for omission	***Don't forget to...***

Spelling

- Year 2 'common exception words' from the National Curriculum: see page 9 of this book for a list of these. These common exception words are highlighted in the Year 2 model texts.

• Words ending in -ful	***bucketful, handful, careful, wonderful***

Checklist

Use this checklist with the Year 2 model texts. See page 7 for more information.

Title statement	
List of equipment or materials	
Sequenced, chronological steps	
Diagrams or illustrations	
Present tense	
Commands	
Detailed information	
Grammar: Coordinating conjunctions	
Grammar: Subordinating conjunctions	
Grammar: Expanded noun phrases	
Grammar: Direct address using 'you'	
Grammar: Adverbials of place	
Punctuation: Question marks	
Punctuation: Commas for lists	
Punctuation: Apostrophes for possession (GDS)	
Punctuation: Apostrophes for omission	
Spelling: Year 2 common exception words	
Words ending in -ful	

Grammarsaurus KS1© Mitch Hudson and Anna Richards 2021

Year 2 model text 1

How to find buried treasure

Ahoy there matey! Are you a helpless pirate searching for your lost treasure? If so, follow these simple instructions so you can be reunited with your prized cargo!

Equipment

- a detailed treasure map
- a spade
- a working compass
- a flask of cold water

Steps to success

1. First, find the treasure map in the captain's quarters and search for the large, red cross in the centre of the desert island.

2. After that, grab a spade from the store cupboard and prepare to row to the island. Ask your most trusted crew members to go with you and beware of dangerous, snapping crocodiles that lurk in the waters!

3. Once you have reached the beach, use your compass to find north and set off in that direction.

4. If your path is blocked with thick bushes, use a sharp knife to cut them down, but remember to be careful.

Grammarsaurus KS1© Mitch Hudson and Anna Richards 2021

5. When you reach the spot next to the tall palm trees where the treasure is buried, use your spade to dig a deep hole. The treasure chest is just below the sand.

6. Finally, drag the treasure chest filled with gold back to the beach. Make sure to row back to the ship sneakily so the captain doesn't see you or he might steal the treasure for himself!

Warning!

Remember to take a break every hour and have a drink of water or you'll get ill.

Grammarsaurus KS1© Mitch Hudson and Anna Richards 2021

Year 2 model text 1: annotated

Dark grey highlights = common exception words

↓→ title statement

How to find buried treasure

↓ present tense

Ahoy there matey! Are you a helpless pirate searching for your lost treasure? If so, follow these simple instructions so you can be reunited with your prized cargo!

second person pronoun ↑ · question mark ↑ · ↑ subordinating conjunction · expanded noun phrase ↗ · ↖ expanded noun phrase

Equipment

↓↑ list of equipment

- a detailed treasure map
  ↑ expanded noun phrase
- a spade
- a working compass
- a flask of cold water

Steps to success

↓↑ sequenced steps

1. First, find the treasure map in the captain's quarters and search for the large, red cross in the centre of the desert island.

↑ imperative · apostrophe for possession ↑ · coordinating conjunction ↑ · comma for list ↗ · adverbial of place ↗ · ↖ adverbial of place

↓↑ sequenced steps

2. After that, grab a spade from the store cupboard and prepare to row to the island. Ask your most trusted crew members to go with you and beware of dangerous, snapping crocodiles that lurk in the waters!

↑ coordinating conjunction · comma for list ↗

↓↑ sequenced steps

3. Once you have reached the beach, use your compass to find north and set off in that direction.

↓↑ sequenced steps

4. If your path is blocked with thick bushes, use a sharp knife to cut them down, but remember to be careful.

↑ expanded noun phrase · word ending in -ful ↑

Grammarsaurus KS1© Mitch Hudson and Anna Richards 2021

↓↑ sequenced steps

5. When you reach the spot next to the tall palm trees where the treasure is buried, use your spade to dig a deep hole. The treasure chest is just below the sand.

↑ subordinating conjunction (When)
detailed information ↗ (The treasure chest is just below the sand.)

↓↑ sequenced steps

6. Finally, drag the treasure chest filled with gold back to the beach. Make sure to row back to the ship sneakily so the captain doesn't see you or he might steal the treasure for himself!

expanded noun phrase ↗ (the treasure chest filled with gold)
apostrophe for omission ↑ (doesn't)

Warning!

Remember to take a break every hour and have a drink of water or you'll get ill.

↑ command (Remember)
↓ statement (you'll get ill.)
coordinating conjunction ↗ (or)
↑ apostrophe for omission (you'll)

Year 2 model text 2

How to build a castle

Do you want the best protection possible? Castles can be easily defended from a harmful attack if they are in the correct position. They should be built on high land with a clear view of the surrounding area to give you a greater awareness of enemy attacks. If you want to avoid disappointment, you must follow these simple steps carefully.

Equipment

- an army of strong, fearless soldiers
- thick blocks of stone
- sharp spades
- long planks of wood

↖portcullis

Steps

1. Firstly, build a moat around the whole of the castle grounds, making sure it is wide and deep. It is easier to shoot any attackers when they are swimming or rowing across the water, but you will still need to keep a careful lookout.

2. After that, use the hard-working soldiers to build high walls with the thick blocks of stone. The high walls will make it harder for attackers to climb over and are a useful defence against the enemy!

3. When finishing the top of the walls, make sure that you use a tooth-shaped design for the battlement. This will help to shelter your soldiers during an attack.

4. Finally, make the main gate or door to the castle. This is normally called a portcullis. Make this from long, sturdy planks of wood and cover it in iron studs. Your enemy won't be able to get through.

Top tip!

Build a round tower rather than a square one because it is harder for ruthless attackers to make round towers collapse! The enemy's plans will be ruined if you do this, and you will be safe.

Grammarsaurus KS1© Mitch Hudson and Anna Richards 2021

Year 2 model text 2: annotated

Dark grey highlights = common exception words

↓→ title statement

How to build a castle

Do you want the best protection possible? Castles can be easily defended from a harmful attack if they are in the correct position. They should be built on high land with a clear view of the surrounding area to give you a greater awareness of enemy attacks. If you want to avoid disappointment, you must follow these simple steps carefully.

question mark ↑

word ending in -ful ↗

↑ subordinating conjunction

expanded noun phrase ↗

↖ expanded noun phrase

↑ second person pronoun

↓↑ list of equipment

Equipment

- an army of strong, fearless soldiers
- thick blocks of stone
- sharp spades
- long planks of wood

↑ comma for list

↖ **portcullis**

Steps

↓↑ sequenced steps

1. Firstly, build a moat around the whole of the castle grounds, making sure it is wide and deep. It is easier to shoot any attackers when they are swimming or rowing across the water, but you will still need to keep a careful lookout.

↑ imperative; adverbial of place ↗; ↖ adverbial of place; ↓ present tense; present tense ↓↗; ↖↓ present tense; ↖ coordinating conjunction

↓↑ sequenced steps

2. After that, use the hard-working soldiers to build high walls with the thick blocks of stone. The high walls will make it harder for attackers to climb over and are a useful defence against the enemy!

↑ expanded noun phrase; coordinating conjunction ↑; ↑ word ending in -ful

↓↑ sequenced steps

3. When finishing the top of the walls, make sure that you use a tooth-shaped design for the battlement. This will help to shelter your soldiers during an attack.

↑ subordinating conjunction; expanded noun phrase ↗; ↖ expanded noun phrase; detailed information ↗; ↖ detailed information; ↖ detailed information

↓↑ sequenced steps

4. Finally, make the main gate or door to the castle. This is normally called a portcullis. Make this from long, sturdy planks of wood and cover it in iron studs. Your enemy won't be able to get through.

↑ expanded noun phrase; detailed information ↗; ↖ detailed information; comma for list ↑; apostrophe for omission ↑

Top tip!

Build a round tower rather than a square one because it is harder for ruthless attackers to make round towers collapse! The enemy's plans will be ruined if you do this, and you will be safe.

↑ expanded noun phrase; apostrophe for possession ↗

Explanation texts

The purpose of an explanation text is to explain to the reader how something works or why something happens.

Tips for teaching children to write explanation texts

- Explanation texts and instructional texts can sometimes be confused. Remind children that explanation texts explain why something happens or how something works whilst instructional texts usually explain how to do something in a step-by-step guide. In terms of the audience, the reader of an instructional text is expected to follow the steps, whereas the reader of an explanation text is looking for general information about a process.

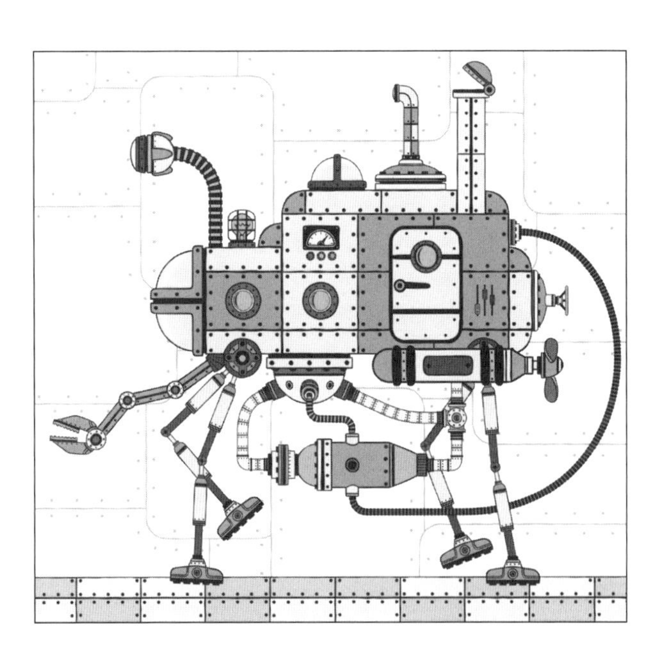

- It is often easier for children to write explanations about something fictional, such as a new invention. This can allow children to focus on the grammar, punctuation and spelling skills rather than getting lost in the details of a real-life topic.

Grammarsaurus KS1© Mitch Hudson and Anna Richards 2021

- Show children different ways to plan an explanation text. Flow charts are useful as they remind children that each step should flow on to the next. A flow chart could be constructed together as a class, for example on a whiteboard. Use arrows to link the different stages of the text. To support further, you might ask the children to record the adverbials of time they will use and write these on the whiteboard between each stage.

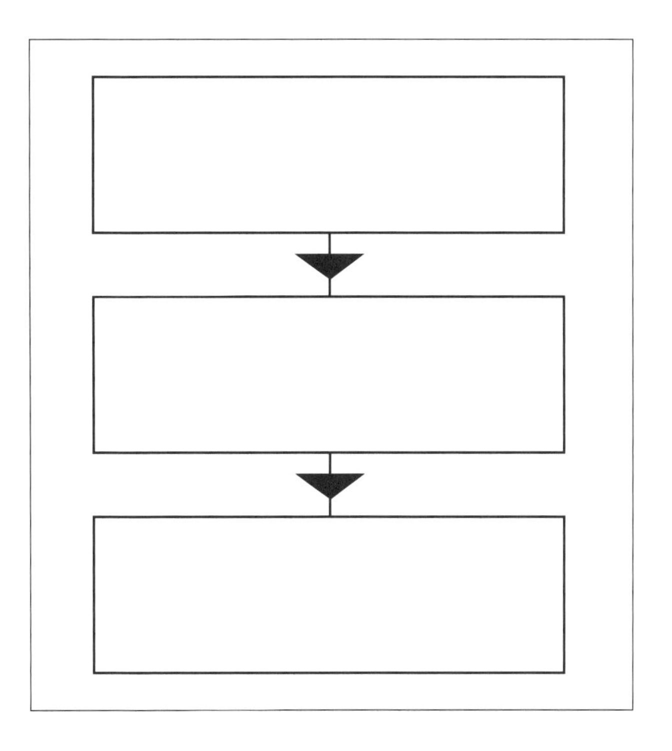

- In addition to or instead of flow charts, younger children or less confident writers could start by ordering pictures showing a process and then labelling each stage rather than writing a whole explanation text straight away.

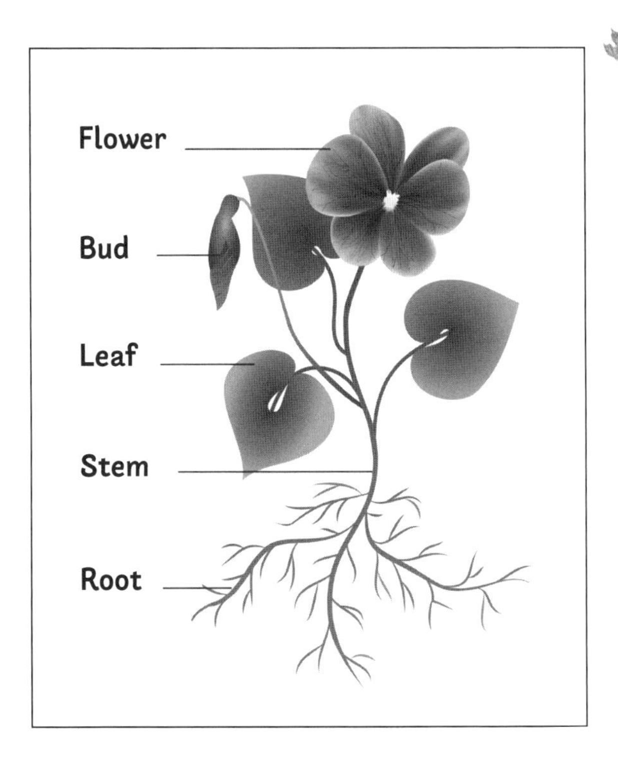

- Remind children that explanations must seem factual (even if the topic is about something fictional), and therefore, their language choices should be technical. Use different discussion activities before writing so that children are confident using the technical vocabulary associated with the topic. These activities might include identifying the different parts of a flower with a partner or placing event cards in the correct order and explaining how they decided on this order.

Year 1 overview

Use this overview and the checklist alongside the Year 1 model text (pages 32 – 35).

Specific features for this text type

• A title phrased as a question	*How is trifle made?*
• An introductory paragraph – say what is going to be explained	*Trifle is a popular dessert, but how many people know how this pudding is made?*
• Paragraphs detailing a process, often in chronological order	
• Facts	*Trifles have three layers.*
• Present tense	*The jelly sets after four hours.* *Sprinkles are added at the end for decoration.*
• Formal language and technical vocabulary	*mould, whip, set, decorate*

The following lists should be used as a tool to help teachers plan where to cover explicit grammar, punctuation and spelling objectives from the National Curriculum Programmes of Study.

Grammar

• Coordinating conjunctions – link ideas with 'and'	*The liquid jelly sets and turns into a solid.*
• Expanded noun phrases – add detail to nouns	*shaped mould* *cubes of jelly*
• Adverbs / adverbials of time	*Next, whipped cream is added.*
• Adverbs / adverbials of place (preposition phrases)	*...added to the top of the trifle.*
• Adverbs / adverbials of manner – say how something is done	*The jelly is removed carefully from the fridge.*

Punctuation

• Question marks – if the title is a question	*How is trifle made?*

Grammarsaurus KS1© Mitch Hudson and Anna Richards 2021

Spelling

- Year 1 'common exception words' from the National Curriculum: see page 9 of this book for a list of these. These common exception words are highlighted in the Year 1 model text.

• Plurals of nouns ending in -s or -es	*packets, boxes*
• Words starting with un-	*unsafe, unclean, untidy*

Checklist

Use this checklist with the Year 1 model text. See page 7 for more information.

Title phrased as a question	
Introductory paragraph	
Paragraphs detailing a process	
Facts	
Present tense	
Formal language and technical vocabulary	
Grammar: Coordinating conjunctions	
Grammar: Expanded noun phrases	
Grammar: Adverbs / adverbials of time	
Grammar: Adverbs / adverbials of place	
Grammar: Adverbs / adverbials of manner	
Punctuation: Question marks	
Spelling: Year 1 common exception words	
Spelling: Plurals of nouns ending in -s or -es	
Spelling: Words starting with un-	

Year 1 model text

How is bread made?

Bread is eaten around the world by many people every day, but do you know how it is made?

To start with, all of the ingredients have to be thoroughly mixed. They are water, flour, yeast and salt. This makes dough.

Seeds or nuts can be added to the dough so that the bread tastes better.

Then the dough is kneaded. It can be made into different shapes and sizes.

Grammarsaurus KS1© Mitch Hudson and Anna Richards 2021

After that, the dough is left to rise fully before it is baked in a hot oven. It is unsafe to touch the bread when it first comes out of the oven.

Did you know that bread was eaten by the Ancient Egyptians 4,000 years ago?

The bread is now ready and it can be sent to the local market.

Year 1 model text: annotated

Dark grey highlights = common exception words

↓title

How is bread made?

question mark ↑

introductory paragraph

Bread is eaten around the
adverbial of place ↗
world by many people every
↖adverbial of place
day, but do you know how it is made?

paragraphs detailing the process

To start with, all of the ingredients have to be thoroughly mixed. They
↑ adverb of manner
are water, flour, yeast and salt.
↑ technical vocabulary
This makes dough.
↑ present tense

Seeds or nuts
↑ plurals ending in -s
can be added to
adverbial of place ↗
the dough so that
↖adverbial of place
the bread tastes better.

↓↑ paragraphs detailing the process

Then the dough is kneaded. It can
↑ adverb of time ↑ technical vocabulary
be made into different shapes
plurals ending -s ↗
and sizes.
↖ plurals ending -s

↓↑ paragraphs detailing the process

After that, the dough is left to rise
↑ adverbial of time
fully before it is baked in a hot oven.
expanded noun phrase ↑
It is unsafe to touch the bread
↑ word beginning with un-
when it first comes out of the oven.

fact

Did you know that bread was eaten by the Ancient Egyptians 4,000 years ago?
↑ adverbial of time

↓↑ paragraphs detailing the process

The bread is now ready and it can
↑ present tense ↑ coordinating conjunction
be sent to the local market.
↑ expanded noun phrase

Year 2 overview

Use this overview and the checklist alongside the Year 2 model texts (pages 38 – 45).

Specific features for this text type

• A title phrased as a question	*How can we keep our teeth clean?*
• An introductory paragraph – say what is going to be explained	*It is important to keep your teeth clean, but how can this be done best?*
• Paragraphs detailing a process, often in chronological order	
• Facts	*Most children have a full set of 20 milk teeth.*
• Present tense	*It is important to brush your teeth twice a day.*
• Formal language and technical vocabulary	*enamel, decay, plaque, molar*

The following lists should be used as a tool to help teachers plan where to cover explicit grammar, punctuation and spelling objectives from the National Curriculum Programmes of Study.

Grammar

• Coordinating conjunctions – link ideas with 'and'	*The brush removes plaque and tartar.*
• Subordinating conjunctions – expand upon independent clauses with 'when' or 'because'	*When a child is around six months old...*
• Expanded noun phrases – add detail to nouns	*the bristles of the brush* *a pea-sized blob*
• Statements – simple facts	*This should last for two minutes.*
• Questions – hook the reader's interest	*How can we keep our teeth clean?*

Punctuation

• Commas for lists	*in books, in newspapers or online*
• Apostrophes for possession (GDS)	*the tooth's enamel*

Grammarsaurus KS1© Mitch Hudson and Anna Richards 2021

Spelling

- Year 2 'common exception words' from the National Curriculum: see page 9 of this book for a list of these. These common exception words are highlighted in the Year 2 model texts.

• Words ending in -ies	*babies, carries, families*
• Comparatives ending in -er	*smaller, longer, cleaner*
• Adverbs ending in -ly (remind children that not all adverbs end with -ly)	*gently, carefully, thoroughly*

Checklist

Use this checklist with the Year 2 model texts. See page 7 for more information.

Title	
Introductory paragraph	
Paragraphs detailing a process	
Facts	
Present tense	
Formal language and technical vocabulary	
Grammar: Coordinating conjunctions	
Grammar: Subordinating conjunctions	
Grammar: Expanded noun phrases	
Grammar: Statements	
Grammar: Questions	
Punctuation: Commas for lists	
Punctuation: Apostrophes for possession (GDS)	
Spelling: Year 2 common exception words	
Spelling: Words ending in -ies	
Spelling: Comparatives ending in -er	
Spelling: Adverbs ending in -ly	

Grammarsaurus KS1© Mitch Hudson and Anna Richards 2021

Year 2 model text 1

How do plants grow?

Everywhere you look, you will see many plants of all shapes, sizes and colours, but do you know how they grow? The lifecycle of a plant is very simple to understand. Each part of a plant has a job that will help it to grow. Read on to find out more.

Most plants start as seeds or bulbs. First, the seed will grow roots. The roots grow downwards into the soil because this helps to secure the plant in the ground. The roots' job is also to **absorb** water and food from the soil. This food is important because it helps the plants to grow.

absorb:

to suck up or to soak up

At the same time, the seed's shoots will grow upwards and then it will grow leaves above the ground. The shoots form a stem.

Grammarsaurus KS1© Mitch Hudson and Anna Richards 2021

After about a week, the seed becomes a seedling. It will grow taller and the leaves will become bigger. The stem carries food from the leaves to the rest of the plant so the flowers can grow. New seeds are made when flowers form! When the new seeds are pollinated, new plants might be able to grow.

When the weather becomes colder, the plant starts to die. The plant will quickly turn brown and the petals or the leaves will soon fall off. Following that, the seeds will fall out of the dead flower and onto the soil. They will replant themselves and the cycle begins again. We call this a lifecycle.

? ***Did you know that plants will only grow well in the right conditions? If the temperature is too hot or too cold, this may stop the plant from growing.***

Year 2 model text 1: annotated

Dark grey highlights = common exception words

↓title

How do plants grow?

introductory paragraph

Everywhere you look, you will see many plants of all shapes, sizes and colours, but do you know how they grow? The lifecycle of a plant is very simple to understand. Each part of a plant has a job that will help it to grow. Read on to find out more.

(comma for list; coordinating conjunction; question; question; expanded noun phrase)

↓↑ paragraphs detailing the process

Most plants start as seeds or bulbs. First, the seed will grow roots. The roots grow downwards into the soil because this helps to secure the plant in the ground. The roots' job is also to **absorb** water and food from the soil. This food is important because it helps the plants to grow.

(technical vocabulary; technical vocabulary; statement; statement; apostrophe for possession; present tense)

absorb:

to suck up or to soak up

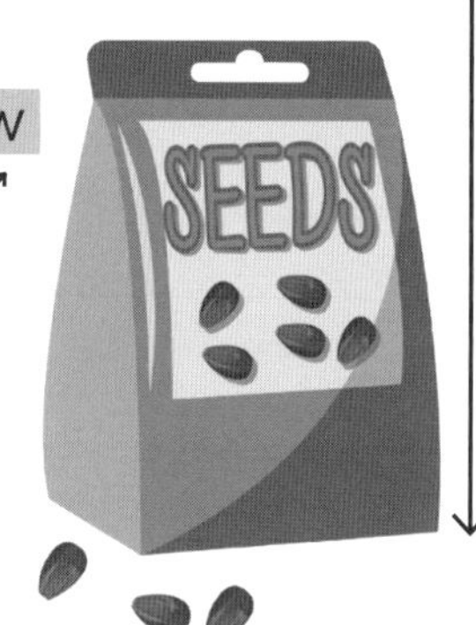

↓↑ paragraphs detailing the process

At the same time, the seed's shoots will grow upwards and then it will grow leaves above the ground. The shoots form a stem.

(expanded noun phrase; expanded noun phrase; coordinating conjunction; formal language; formal language)

Grammarsaurus KS1© Mitch Hudson and Anna Richards 2021

↓↑ paragraphs detailing the process

After about a week, the seed becomes a seedling. It will grow taller and the leaves will become bigger. The stem carries food from the leaves to the rest of the plant so the flowers can grow. New seeds are made when flowers form! When the new seeds are pollinated, new plants might be able to grow.

↑ comparative ending in -er (taller)
↑ comparative ending in -er (bigger)
↑ word ending in -ies (carries)

↓↑ paragraphs detailing the process

When the weather becomes colder, the plant starts to die. The plant will quickly turn brown and the petals or the leaves will

↑ subordinating conjunction (When)
↑ comparative ending in -er (colder)
↑ adverb ending in -ly (quickly)

↓↑ paragraphs detailing the process

soon fall off. Following that, the seeds will fall out of the dead flower and onto the soil. They will replant themselves and the cycle begins again.

expanded noun phrase ↗ (the dead)
↖ expanded noun phrase (flower)

↓ statement

We call this a lifecycle.

↑ technical vocabulary (a lifecycle)

? ***Did you know that plants will only grow well in the right conditions? If the temperature is too hot or too cold, this may stop the plant from growing.***

facts ↗ (plants)
↖ facts (will only grow well in)
↖ facts (the right conditions)
↑ subordinating conjunction (If)

Year 2 model text 2

How do food chains work?

There are many different food chains around us, but a food chain will always start with the sun because this is where plants get their energy from.

Plants make their food in their leaves through a process called photosynthesis. Plants are then eaten by animals. Usually, these animals are smaller in size like caterpillars, snails and rabbits, but larger animals like cows and horses also graze on plants. When an animal is at the start of the food chain, they are known as primary consumers.

Following that, primary consumers are hunted and become food for other animals. This continues with more animals so that a food chain is created. The development of the food chain relies on there being enough living things at every level.

Look at the example of the food chain. It uses helpful arrows to show the direction of the chain. In this food chain, the grass makes food from the sun's energy which is then eaten by the cow. After that, these cows are eaten by humans. When the food chain reaches humans, it stops because no one eats humans! We are at the top of the food chain. Can you think of any other food chains where humans are at the top?

? ***Did you know that an animal that only eats plants is called a herbivore, an animal that only eats other animals is called a carnivore and an omnivore is an animal that eats both plants and animals?***

? ***Did you know that food chains happen on land and in water?***

Key words:

- **producers:** living things that make or produce their own food
- **consumers:** animals that eat other living things
- **predators:** animals that hunt and eat other animals
- **prey:** animals that get eaten by predators

Year 2 model text 2: annotated

Dark grey highlights = common exception words

↓title

How do food chains work?

introductory paragraph

There are many different food chains around us, but a food chain will always start with the sun because this is where plants get their energy from.

coordinating conjunction ↑ (but)
↑ subordinating conjunction (because)

↓paragraphs detailing the process

Plants make their food in their leaves through a process called photosynthesis. Plants are then eaten by animals. Usually, these animals are smaller in size like caterpillars, snails and rabbits, but larger animals like cows and horses also graze on plants. When an animal is at the start of the food chain, they are known as primary consumers.

↑ technical vocabulary (photosynthesis)
formal language ↗ (Plants are then eaten by animals.)
↖ formal language
↑ adverb ending in -ly (Usually)
↑ comparative ending in -er (smaller)
↑ comma for list
↑ technical vocabulary (primary consumers)

↓↑ paragraphs detailing the process

Following that, primary consumers are hunted and become food for other animals. This continues with

↑ coordinating conjunction (and)

Grammarsaurus KS1© Mitch Hudson and Anna Richards 2021

↓↑ paragraphs detailing the process

more animals so that a food chain is created. The development of the food chain relies on there being enough living things at every level.

↑ subordinating conjunction; formal language; formal language; word ending in -ies

↓↑ paragraphs detailing the process

Look at the example of the food chain. It uses helpful arrows to show the direction of the chain. In this food chain, the grass makes

expanded noun phrase; expanded noun phrase

↓↑ paragraphs detailing the process

food from the sun's energy which is then eaten by the cow. After that, these cows are eaten by humans. When the food chain reaches humans, it stops because no one eats humans! We are at the top of the food chain. Can you think of any other food chains where humans are at the top?

↑ apostrophe for possession; present tense; statement; statement; question; question; question

facts

Did you know that an animal that only eats plants is called a herbivore, an animal that only eats other animals is called a carnivore and an omnivore is an animal that eats both plants and animals?

↑ question; technical vocabulary; technical vocabulary; technical vocabulary

facts

Did you know that food chains happen on land and in water?

Key words:

↑↓ technical vocabulary

- **producers:** living things that make or produce their own food
  ↑ coordinating conjunction
- **consumers:** animals that eat other living things
- **predators:** animals that hunt and eat other animals
- **prey:** animals that get eaten by predators

Non-chronological reports

The purpose of a non-chronological report is to document and store information about a topic.

Tips for teaching children to write non-chronological reports

- Children can find it easier to write a report based on their real-life experiences. When possible, consider how you could enable children to see or experience what they are going to write about. For example, could they visit a castle before writing about it?

- It can sometimes be difficult for children to focus on their writing skills if they are thinking too much about the content. In this case, using a made-up context can allow children to focus on the grammar, punctuation and spelling rather than the factual details of a real-life event. For example, could they write a report about their own mythical creature or a new character for a book they have read?

- If you are using a real-life stimulus, children will need to know key factual information to include in their report. Ask children to research a specific area and then 'interview' each other about the different topics to find out information in a more interesting way. For example, you might ask children to take notes whilst on a school trip or retrieve relevant information from simple books or information leaflets.

- To ensure that children are grouping relevant information in paragraphs, give children a paragraph to read and ask them to guess what the subheading might be. For example, can they read a paragraph about food an animal likes to eat and guess that the subheading is 'diet'? After they have written a paragraph, ask them to look at it again and think about whether a reader would be able to guess the subheading.

- Help children find technical vocabulary to use in their writing. If children are writing about the appearance of an animal, for example, display an image of an animal and label the body parts with technical vocabulary, such as 'sharp talons' and 'large wings'. Children could refer to these labels during independent writing sessions.

Year 1 overview

Use this overview and the checklist alongside the Year 1 model text (pages 50 – 53).

Specific features for this text type

• A heading – introduce the topic	*Birds of prey*
• A brief introduction – general information	*Across the world, people are fascinated by...*
• Subheadings – organise the text into categories	
• Technical vocabulary	*talons, beak, feathers*
• Pictures and captions	
• Third person – formal	*Eagles like to live near water.*
• Statements giving factual information (any tense)	*Owls hunt at night.*

The following lists should be used as a tool to help teachers plan where to cover explicit grammar, punctuation and spelling objectives from the National Curriculum Programmes of Study.

Grammar

• Coordinating conjunctions – link ideas with 'and'	*feathers and sharp talons*
• Adverbs / adverbials of place – say where the subject of the report is located	*in the countryside in Scotland* *under the tree*
• Expanded noun phrases – add detail to nouns with 'under', 'around', 'next to', 'above' and 'with'	*large mouths with sharp, curved beaks*

Punctuation

• Capital letters for proper nouns – for example, for geographical locations	*Atlantic Ocean*

Grammarsaurus KS1© Mitch Hudson and Anna Richards 2021

Spelling

- Year 1 'common exception words' from the National Curriculum: see page 9 of this book for a list of these. These common exception words are highlighted in the Year 1 model text.
- Plurals of nouns ending in -s or -es — *wings, feathers, bushes*

Checklist

Use this checklist with the Year 1 model text. See page 7 for more information.

Heading	
Brief introduction	
Subheadings	
Technical vocabulary	
Pictures and captions	
Third person – formal	
Statements giving factual information	
Grammar: Coordinating conjunctions	
Grammar: Adverbs / adverbials of place	
Grammar: Expanded noun phrases	
Punctuation: Capital letters for proper nouns	
Spelling: Year 1 common exception words	
Spelling: Plurals of nouns ending in -s or -es	

Grammarsaurus KS1© Mitch Hudson and Anna Richards 2021

Arctic animals

The Arctic is very cold so animals have had to change to live there. Many animals live there, but it can be hard. It is very dark in the winter and very light in the summer.

Here are some animals that live in the Arctic.

Polar bears

Polar bears can swim a long way and they are also very large. They catch and eat a lot of food between April and July. They do this so they do not have to eat in winter.

↓ **polar bear**

They have to find somewhere to do this. Their burrows are under the ground to be safe. They can be found in Alaska, Canada and Russia.

There are many other animals that live in the Arctic. Do you want to find out more now that you have read about these amazing creatures?

Arctic wolves

Arctic wolves have thick fur coats to help protect them from the cold. The fur gets thicker in the colder months. Arctic wolves are smaller than other wolves.

Arctic ground squirrels

Some animals like the Arctic ground squirrel hibernate during the winter months.

↓ Arctic ground squirrel

Year 1 model text: annotated

Dark grey highlights = common exception words

↓ heading

Arctic animals

brief introduction

The Arctic is very cold so animals have had to change to live there. Many animals live there, but it can be hard. It is very dark in the winter and very light in the summer.

factual statement ↗ ↖ factual statement — coordinating conjunction ↑

Here are some animals that live in the Arctic.

expanded noun phrase ↘ ↙ expanded noun phrase

↓ subheading

Polar bears

↑ plural ending in -s

Polar bears can swim a long way and they are also very large. They catch and eat a lot of food between April and July. They do this so they do not have to eat in winter.

↑ third person ↑ coordinating conjunction ↑ capitals for proper nouns

↓ **polar bear**

Grammarsaurus KS1© Mitch Hudson and Anna Richards 2021

Arctic wolves

Arctic wolves have thick fur coats

to help protect them from the

cold. The fur gets thicker in the

expanded noun phrase ↗

colder months. Arctic wolves are

↖ expanded noun phrase

smaller than other wolves.

Arctic ground squirrels

↑ plural ending in -s

Some animals like the Arctic

ground squirrel hibernate

↑ technical vocabulary

during the winter months.

They have to find somewhere

↓ technical vocabulary

to do this. Their burrows are

↑ third person ⟶

↓ adverbial of place

under the ground to be safe.

↓ factual statement ⟶

They can be found in Alaska,

↓ factual statement ⟶

Canada and Russia.

plural ending in -s ↓

There are many other animals

↓ adverbial of place ⟶

that live in the Arctic. Do you

↑ capital for proper noun

want to find out more now

that you have read about

these amazing creatures?

↑ expanded noun phrase

↓ Arctic ground squirrel

Year 2 overview

Use this overview and the checklist alongside the Year 2 model texts (pages 56 – 63).

Specific features for this text type

• A heading – introduce the topic	*Football clubs in England*
• A brief introduction – general information	*Football is a popular sport in England...*
• Subheadings – organise the text into categories	
• Technical vocabulary	*stadium, match, season, penalty*
• Pictures and captions	
• Third person – formal	*The most popular team is...*
• Statements giving factual information (any tense)	*There are 20 teams in the league.*

The following lists should be used as a tool to help teachers plan where to cover explicit grammar, punctuation and spelling objectives from the National Curriculum Programmes of Study.

Grammar

• Coordinating conjunctions – 'but', 'or' or 'and'	*red or yellow card*
• Subordinating conjunctions – expand upon independent clauses with 'if', 'when' or 'because'	*When the referee blows the whistle...*
• Expanded noun phrases – add detail to nouns with 'of', 'from', 'under', 'around', 'surrounding', 'next to', 'above' and 'with'	*the spectators in the stadium* *the penalty spot*
• Present progressive – use this tense with 'when'	*When the team is playing...*
• Statements – simple facts	*There are 11 players in a team.*
• Questions – invite the reader to know more	*Have you ever wondered how...?*
• Commands / imperative – use these with 'if'	*If you're in the penalty box, watch out...*

Punctuation

• Capital letters for proper nouns	*Manchester, England, Premier League*
• Commas for lists	*socks, shorts and a t-shirt*
• Apostrophes for possession (GDS)	*the referee's whistle*

Grammarsaurus KS1© Mitch Hudson and Anna Richards 2021

Spelling

- Year 2 'common exception words' from the National Curriculum: see page 9 of this book for a list of these. These common exception words are highlighted in the Year 2 model texts.

• Comparatives ending in -er	*faster, quicker, greater*
• Superlatives ending in -est	*fastest, biggest, greatest*
• Words ending in -ful	*beautiful, eventful, joyful*
• Words ending in -less	*careless, fearless*

Checklist

Use this checklist with the Year 2 model texts. See page 7 for more information.

Heading and subheadings	
Brief introduction	
Technical vocabulary	
Pictures and captions	
Third person – formal	
Statements giving factual information	
Grammar: Coordinating conjunctions	
Grammar: Subordinating conjunctions	
Grammar: Expanded noun phrases	
Grammar: Present progressive	
Grammar: Statements	
Grammar: Questions	
Grammar: Commands / imperative	
Punctuation: Capital letters for proper nouns	
Punctuation: Commas for lists	
Punctuation: Apostrophes for possession (GDS)	
Spelling: Year 2 common exception words	
Spelling: Comparatives and superlatives	
Spelling: Words ending in -ful	
Spelling: Words ending in -less	

Grammarsaurus KS1© Mitch Hudson and Anna Richards 2021

Year 2 model text 1

Marine mammals

Have you ever wondered how marine mammals differ from other mammals? Most of these animals have a thick layer of blubber because it helps to keep them warm in the cold sea.

Read on to find out more.

Seals

Seals can dive very deep underwater and some can stay there for up to two hours. To communicate with each other, these amazing creatures use clicking noises or some use trilling sounds.

↓ seal pup

Sea lions

These wonderful mammals walk on land using all four flippers, but they only use their front flippers to swim. Sea lions can swim very fast in short bursts, but most of the time they swim at a much slower speed of around 11 miles per hour. People sometimes confuse these creatures with seals, but it is easy

? ***Did you know that male seals are called bulls, females are called cows and babies are called pups?***

Grammarsaurus KS1© Mitch Hudson and Anna Richards 2021

to tell the difference between them. Sea lions are brown, bark loudly and have ear flaps on their heads. Seals have small flippers, wriggle on their bellies on land, and you can't see their ears.

↓ sea lion

Dolphins

Dolphins are very intelligent animals that spend a lot of time under the water, but come to the surface to breathe using a blowhole on the top of their head. They are remarkable creatures that use sonar when

↓ dolphin

they are hunting their prey. Many people think dolphins are the friendliest and most playful animals of the sea!

Sadly, many harmless marine mammals are endangered, and there are threats to most of their populations, such as hunting, pollution and loss of habitat, so organisations like Greenpeace work hard to protect them.

These aren't the only marine mammals. Others include sea otters, walruses, whales, manatees and polar bears.

Grammarsaurus KS1© Mitch Hudson and Anna Richards 2021

Year 2 model text 1: annotated

Dark grey highlights = common exception words

↓heading

Marine mammals

brief introduction

Have you ever wondered how marine mammals differ from other mammals? Most of these animals have a thick layer of blubber because it helps to keep them warm in the cold sea.

technical vocabulary ↗ ↖technical vocabulary ↑subordinating conjunction

↓command

Read on to find out more.

Seals

Seals can dive very deep underwater and some can stay there for up to two hours. To communicate with each other, these amazing creatures use clicking noises or some use trilling sounds.

↑coordinating conjunction ↑expanded noun phrase ↑coordinating conjunction

↓ **seal pup**

↓subheading

Sea lions

↓expanded noun phrase

These wonderful mammals walk on land using all four flippers, but they only use their front flippers to swim. Sea lions can swim very fast in short bursts, but most of the time they swim at a much slower speed of around 11 miles per hour. People sometimes confuse these creatures with seals, but it is easy

↑word ending in -ful present tense ↑ coordinating conjunction ↑ ↓factual ↓factual ↓factual ↓factual comparative with -er ↑ ↓third person

Did you know that male seals are called bulls, females are called cows and babies are called pups?

↑question ↑comma for list

Grammarsaurus KS1© Mitch Hudson and Anna Richards 2021

to tell the difference between them. Sea lions are brown, bark loudly and have ear flaps on their heads. Seals have small flippers, wriggle on their bellies on land, and you can't see their ears.

comma for list ↑

↓ **sea lion**

Dolphins

Dolphins are very intelligent animals that spend a lot of time under the water,but come to the surface to breathe using a blowhole on the top of their head. They are remarkable creatures that use sonar when

statement ↗ ↖ statement
↑ technical vocabulary
subordinating conjunction ↑

↓ **dolphin**

they are hunting their prey. Many people think dolphins are the friendliest and most playful animals of the sea!

↑ present progressive
↑ superlative with -est ↑ word ending in -ful

Sadly, many harmless marine mammals are endangered, and there are threats to most of their populations, such as hunting, pollution and loss of habitat, so organisations like Greenpeace work hard to protect them.

↑ word ending in -less
↑ technical vocabulary
coordinating conjunction ↑
capital letter for proper noun ↑

These aren't the only marine mammals. Others include sea otters, walruses, whales, manatees and polar bears.

↖ ↑ ↗ commas for lists

Grammarsaurus KS1© Mitch Hudson and Anna Richards 2021

Kings and queens

Kings and queens have played an important role in history as they are powerful people who rule countries. Kings and queens are also called 'monarchs'. Here is some information about some of the most famous monarchs of England and Great Britain.

↑ Henry VIII

Henry VIII

King Henry VIII was crowned when he was 17 years old in 1509 and he reigned until he died in 1547. He is one of English history's most famous kings. He is remembered for being rebellious, greedy and having six wives.

Henry wanted to have a son so that his prince could be king one day. His third wife, Jane Seymour, did have a baby boy called Edward, who became king when Henry died, but sadly he would not live to see adulthood.

Headless queens

King Henry VIII was unhappy with many of his wives, so cruelly he had their heads chopped off or divorced them.

Grammarsaurus KS1© Mitch Hudson and Anna Richards 2021

His second wife, Anne Boleyn, had her head cut off in 1536. Her ghost is said to haunt the Tower of London, where she was killed.

Queen Victoria's empire

The Victorian Era is named after Queen Victoria, who ruled for a very long time. During this time, the British Empire was very powerful and at one point ruled a quarter of the world's countries, including India.

← Queen Victoria

Queen Elizabeth II and her record-breaking reign

Queen Elizabeth II became the Queen of England in 1953 after her father, King George VI, died. Her coronation was the first to be shown on television. It was watched by millions of people!

In 2015, she became the longest-reigning monarch in British history, and this record beat her great-great-grandmother, Queen Victoria, who reigned for 63 years.

What is a coronation?

When a person is made king or queen, there is a special event called a coronation.

← The crown jewels

Year 2 model text 2: annotated

Dark grey highlights = common exception words

↓heading

Kings and queens

brief introduction

Kings and queens have played an important role in history as they are powerful people who rule countries. Kings and queens are also called 'monarchs'. Here is some information about some of the most famous monarchs of England and Great Britain.

factual information ↗

↖ factual information

↑ Henry VIII

Henry VIII

↑ subheading

King Henry VIII was crowned when he was 17 years old in 1509 and he reigned until he died in 1547. He is one of English history's most famous kings. He is remembered for being rebellious, greedy and having six wives.

↑ capitals for proper nouns

coordinating conjunction ↑

↑ technical vocabulary

apostrophe for possession ↑

Henry wanted to have a son so that his prince could be king one day. His third wife, Jane Seymour, did have a baby boy called Edward, who became king when Henry died, but sadly he would not live to see adulthood.

Headless queens

↑ word ending in -less

King Henry VIII was unhappy with many of his wives, so cruelly he had their heads chopped off or divorced them.

coordinating conjunction ↑

Grammarsaurus KS1© Mitch Hudson and Anna Richards 2021

His second wife, Anne Boleyn, had her head cut off in 1536. Her ghost is said to haunt the Tower of London, where she was killed.

statement

Queen Victoria's empire

↑ apostrophe for possession

The Victorian Era is named after Queen Victoria, who ruled for a very long time. During this time, the British Empire was very powerful and at one point ruled a quarter of the world's countries, including India.

↑ word ending in 'ful'
↓ expanded noun phrase
↑ apostrophe for possession
↑ capital for proper noun

← **Queen Victoria**

Queen Elizabeth II and her record-breaking reign

↑ expanded noun phrase

Queen Elizabeth II became the Queen of England in 1953 after her father, King George VI, died. Her coronation was the first to be shown on television. It was watched by millions of people!

↑ technical vocabulary
↑ plural ending in -s

In 2015, she became the longest-reigning monarch in British history, and this record beat her great-great-grandmother, Queen Victoria, who reigned for 63 years.

comparative ending in 'est' ↑
↑ technical vocabulary

What is a coronation?

↑ question

When a person is made king or queen, there is a special event called a coronation.

↑ subordinating conjunction
expanded noun phrase ↗
↖ expanded noun phrase

← **The crown jewels**

Grammarsaurus KS1© Mitch Hudson and Anna Richards 2021

Recounts: diary entries

The purpose of a diary entry is to share a personal account of an event.

Tips for teaching children to write diary entries

- Children can find it easier to write about their real-life experiences. When possible, consider how you could enable children to see or experience what they are going to write a diary entry about. For example, could they visit the seaside or a park before writing about these places?

- The use of role play can be really effective when teaching children about this text type. Ask an adult to dress up as the character you are going to invite the children to write about, for example Florence Nightingale. Then let the children ask questions about an event in that character's life. You could prompt them with a question like, 'Did you ever meet Mary Seacole?' The children can take notes based on the interview before writing a diary entry in role as that character.

Grammarsaurus KS1© Mitch Hudson and Anna Richards 2021

- Recounts don't always have to be long. Think about ways that people recount what they've done, other than by writing diaries. Postcards are a great way for children to write shorter recounts as they still require children to use the key features of a recount, including writing in the past tense and in the first person.

- Consider providing photographs to remind children of the events that they are going to write about. For younger or less confident writers, you could ask them to order the pictures you provide, before writing a sentence about what happened in chronological order.

- Teach the children how to show the emotion of the writer rather than describing it. For example, instead of 'I was scared…' share alternatives that show a character's fear in a different way, such as 'my fingers trembled' or 'my heart pounded'. This is an effective way to support children in developing inference skills as readers, too.

Year 1 overview

Use this overview and the checklist alongside the Year 1 model text (pages 68 – 69).

Specific features for this text type

Feature	Example
• Date – say when the account was written	
• Salutation (optional)	*Dear Diary...*
• Chronological order – sequenced paragraphs	*This morning, yesterday, last week...*
• Past tense	*went, sailed, walked, visited*
• First person – informal	*I went to...*
• A mixture of facts and opinions	*The park is close to my house.* *Visiting the circus was exciting.*
• Rhetorical questions	*Guess what he told me?*
• Sign off (optional)	*I will write again tomorrow.*

The following lists should be used as a tool to help teachers plan where to cover explicit grammar, punctuation and spelling objectives from the National Curriculum Programmes of Study.

Grammar

Feature	Example
• Coordinating conjunctions – link ideas with 'and'	*I travelled on a ship and it felt like I was on a big adventure!*
• Adverbs / adverbials of time – say when events took place	*That evening,* *The next morning,*
• Adverbs / adverbials of place – say where events took place	*the countryside in Wales*
• Expanded noun phrases – add detail to nouns	*a long bus ride* *a stall with lots of sweets*

Punctuation

Feature	Example
• Capital letters for proper nouns	*Bournemouth*
• Question marks	*What am I going to do tomorrow?*

Grammarsaurus KS1© Mitch Hudson and Anna Richards 2021

Spelling

- Year 1 'common exception words' from the National Curriculum: see page 9 of this book for a list of these. These common exception words are highlighted in the Year 1 model texts.

• Words ending in -ed – for example, when teaching the past tense	***climbed, walked, jumped, changed, improved***
• Plurals of nouns ending in -s	***friends, animals***

Checklist

Use this checklist with the Year 1 model text. See page 7 for more information.

Date	
Salutation	
Chronological order	
Past tense	
First person - informal	
Facts and opinions	
Rhetorical questions	
Sign off	
Grammar: Coordinating conjunctions	
Grammar: Adverbs / adverbials of time	
Grammar: Adverbs / adverbials of place	
Grammar: Expanded noun phrases	
Punctuation: Capital letters for proper nouns	
Punctuation: Question marks	
Spelling: Year 1 common exception words	
Spelling: Words ending in -ed	
Spelling: Plurals of nouns ending in -s	

Grammarsaurus KS1© Mitch Hudson and Anna Richards 2021

Year 1 model text

School trip to the seaside

Tuesday 14th September

Dear Diary,

Today, I went with my class to Southsea for a school trip! All of my friends were there with me. We had so much fun.

First, we walked to the seafront. It was very cold so we wore our coats.

At the beach, we collected pretty shells and put them in buckets. I found a big one and Jenny found a smaller one.

Next, we drew some pictures of the waves. They were very large! It was very exciting.

Then, we ate our tasty lunch on the sand. We sat on a blanket and the teachers sat on chairs.

Soon, it was time to go back to school. Where had the time gone?

What a great day we had!

Love,

Lucy

Grammarsaurus KS1© Mitch Hudson and Anna Richards 2021

Year 1 model text: annotated

School trip to the seaside

Tuesday 14th September
↑ date

Dear Diary,
↑ salutation

Today, I went with my class to Southsea for a school trip! All of my friends were there with me. We had so much fun.
↑ past tense — capital for proper noun ↑ — ↑ expanded noun phrase — ↑ plural of noun

chronological order

First, we walked to the seafront. It was very cold so we wore our coats.
↑ adverb of time — ↖ word ending in 'ed' — ↑ fact

At the beach, we collected pretty shells and put them in buckets.
↑ adverbial of place — ↑ word ending in -ed

I found a big one and Jenny found a smaller one.
↑ coordinating conjunction

Next, we drew some pictures of the waves. They were very large! It was very exciting.
↑ expanded noun phrase

Then, we ate our tasty lunch on the sand. We sat on a blanket and the teachers sat on chairs.
past tense ↑ — ↑ opinion — first person ↑ — ↑ adverbial of place — ↑ coordinating conjunction — ↑ plural ending in -s

Soon, it was time to go back to school. Where had the time gone?
↑ rhetorical question

What a great day we had!

Love,
↑ sign off

Lucy
↑ capital for proper noun

Year 2 overview

Use this overview and the checklist alongside the Year 2 model texts (pages 72 – 79).

Specific features for this text type

• Dates – say when the account was written	
• Salutation (optional)	*Dear Diary,*
• Chronological order – sequenced paragraphs	
• Past tense	*This morning, yesterday, last week, last month...*
• First person – informal	*I looked after injured soldiers.*
• A mixture of facts and opinions	
• Rhetorical questions	*Would things get any better?* *Who else could help?*
• Sign off (optional)	

The following lists should be used as a tool to help teachers plan where to cover explicit grammar, punctuation and spelling objectives from the National Curriculum Programmes of Study.

Grammar

• Coordinating conjunctions – link ideas with 'but', 'so', 'and' or 'or'	*I opened a hotel for the sick soldiers, but it wasn't like a normal hotel!*
• Subordinating conjunctions – expand upon independent clauses with 'when', 'whilst', 'before' or 'after'	*I had to call for help before the man got any sicker.*
• Adverbs / adverbials of time	*Later that day,* *Suddenly,*
• Adverbs / adverbials of place	*beside the hospital bed*
• Expanded noun phrases – add detail to nouns	*a soldier with an awful wound on his chest*

Punctuation

• Exclamation marks	*What a frightening experience it was for us all!*
• Commas – for lists	*The hospital was busy with patients, nurses and doctors.*

Grammarsaurus KS1© Mitch Hudson and Anna Richards 2021

• Apostrophes for omission	*It wasn't my fault.*
• Apostrophes for possession (GDS)	*The patient's breathing was slow.*

Spelling

- Year 2 'common exception words' from the National Curriculum: see page 9 of this book for a list of these. These common exception words are highlighted in the Year 2 model texts.

• Words ending in -ed – for example, when teaching the past tense	***dressed, wounded, spotted***

Checklist

Use this checklist with the Year 2 model texts. See page 7 for more information.

Date	
Salutation	
Chronological order	
Past tense	
First person – informal	
Facts and opinions	
Rhetorical questions	
Sign off	
Grammar: Coordinating conjunctions	
Grammar: Subordinating conjunctions	
Grammar: Adverbs / adverbials of time	
Grammar: Adverbs / adverbials of place	
Grammar: Expanded noun phrases	
Punctuation: Exclamation marks	
Punctuation: Commas for lists	
Punctuation: Apostrophes for omission	
Punctuation: Apostrophes for possession (GDS)	
Spelling: Year 2 common exception words	
Spelling: Words ending in -ed	

Year 2 model text 1

A pirate's life

Day 1 – 21.05.1806

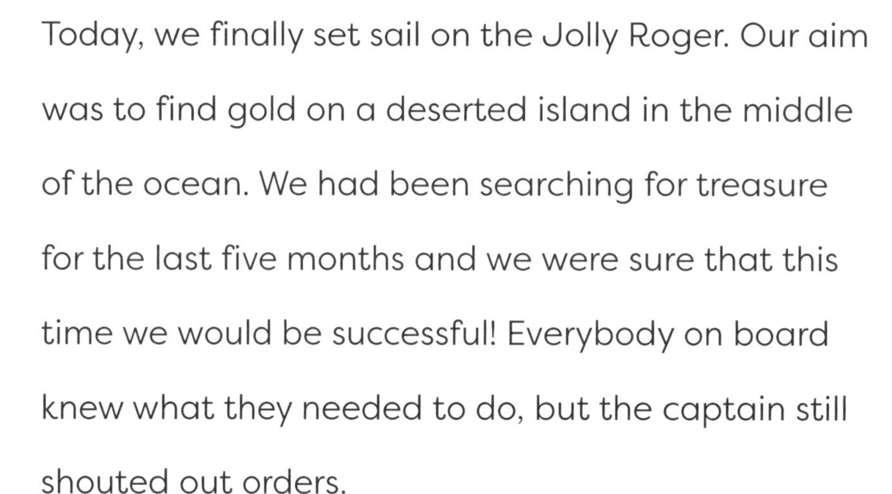

Today, we finally set sail on the Jolly Roger. Our aim was to find gold on a deserted island in the middle of the ocean. We had been searching for treasure for the last five months and we were sure that this time we would be successful! Everybody on board knew what they needed to do, but the captain still shouted out orders.

Day 2 – 22.05.1806

It was a beautiful morning when we woke up. In the late morning, the cabin boy shouted to say that he had seen land ahead. Nobody believed him because he's always saying that he's seen things which aren't really there. The captain had to climb the rigging to see if the cabin boy was telling the truth. Had we really found land so soon? We had! What an exciting day this was!

Grammarsaurus KS1© Mitch Hudson and Anna Richards 2021

Day 3 – 23.05.1806

In the early hours of the morning, we started to prepare for our trip onto the island. We packed a treasure map, a shovel and some water. The captain steered our little rowing boat towards the shore. We jumped into the cold water and headed up the path into the wild jungle.

Day 4 – 24.05.1806

It took a whole day for us to find the site of the treasure or where we thought the gold should be! The captain called to us to start digging. Were we finally going to be rich?

Soon, the ship's cook hit something hard.
It was a chest!

Year 2 model text 1: annotated

Dark grey highlights = common exception words

A pirate's life

Day 1 – 21.05.1806

↑ date

Today, we finally set sail on the Jolly Roger. Our aim was to find gold on a deserted island in the middle of the ocean. We had been searching for treasure for the last five months and we were sure that this time we would be successful! Everybody on board knew what they needed to do, but the captain still shouted out orders.

Annotations: ↑ fact (we finally set sail on the Jolly Roger); adverbial of place (in the middle of the ocean); ↑ coordinating conjunction (and); ↑ past tense (knew); ↑ coordinating conjunction (but)

chronological order

Day 2 – 22.05.1806

It was a beautiful morning when we woke up. In the late morning, the cabin boy shouted to say that he had seen land ahead. Nobody believed him because he's always saying that he's seen things which aren't really there. The captain had to climb the rigging to see if the cabin boy was telling the truth. Had we really found land so soon? We had! What an exciting day this was!

Annotations: ↑ opinion (It was a beautiful morning); subordinating conjunction ↑ (when); adverbial of time (In the late morning); ↑ word ending in -ed (shouted); subordinating conjunction ↑ (because); ↑ apostrophe for omission (he's); apostrophe for omission ↑ (aren't); ↑ subordinating conjunction (if); rhetorical question ↑ (Had we really found land so soon?); ↑ exclamation mark (We had!)

Grammarsaurus KS1© Mitch Hudson and Anna Richards 2021

Day 3 – 23.05.1806

In the early hours of the morning, we started to
↑ adverbial of time ↑ first person
prepare for our trip onto the island. We packed
↑ adverbial of place
a treasure map, a shovel and some water. The
↑ comma for list
captain steered our little rowing boat towards
↑ expanded noun phrase
the shore. We jumped into the cold water and
↑ word ending in -ed
headed up the path into the wild jungle.

Day 4 – 24.05.1806

It took a whole day for us to find the site of the
↑ first person
treasure or where we thought the gold should be!
↑ coordinating conjunction
The captain called to us to start digging. Were we
rhetorical question ↗
finally going to be rich?
↖ rhetorical question

Soon, the ship's cook hit something hard.
↑ apostrophe for possession
It was a chest!

Grammarsaurus KS1© Mitch Hudson and Anna Richards 2021

Year 2 model text 2

Antarctic adventures

15th December 1911

Dear Diary,

Yesterday, after years of hard work and a great amount of effort, we finally reached the South Pole and beat our British competitors. What a fantastic adventure this has been!

Before our trip, one of my crew members had a wonderful idea to improve our sleds. What was his great idea? He made the sleds lighter to make it easier to pull them! The man is a genius, and he definitely helped us save time and energy.

Our trip began in early January when we changed our plans at the last minute to head to the South Pole rather than the North Pole. We altered our plans because another team of explorers had already reached the North Pole.

Eventually, we arrived at the Bay of Whales in Antarctica on 14th January. Quickly, we set up camp and started preparing everything we were going to need if we were going to be successful on our mission.

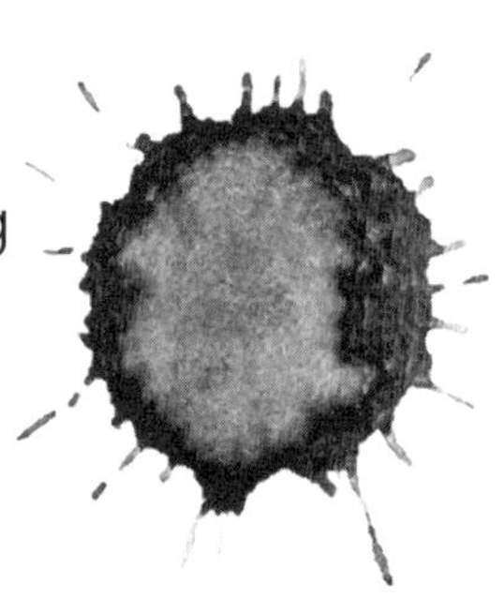

Grammarsaurus KS1© Mitch Hudson and Anna Richards 2021

As soon as we were fully prepared, it was time to set off. It was now mid-April. Our aim was to reach the South Pole within ten months and we were sure we would be able to achieve our goal. We wanted to arrive by October, but we agreed that it might take longer if the weather turned bad. This is exactly what happened on our first attempt. Was this enough to put us off our task? Of course not!

When the weather had improved, we set out again and made a second attempt with a much smaller team. This time, we travelled with five people, four sleds and fifty-two dogs. To start with, we travelled quickly. But soon we had to slow down when we reached deep, dangerous crevasses.

Finally, after we'd completed nearly two months of difficult travelling, we reached the South Pole on 14th December. I was close to tears because I was so pleased to have made it!
I planted the Norwegian flag in the ground, so I could prove we'd been there. It was all worth it for we had beaten the British team's attempt.

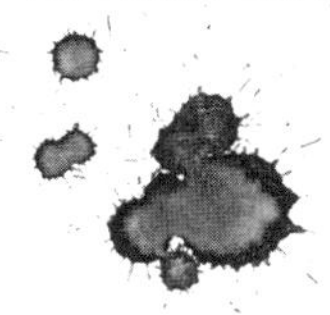

Roald Amundsen

Year 2 model text 2: annotated

Dark grey highlights = common exception words

Antarctic adventures

↓ date
15th December 1911

Dear Diary,
↑ salutation

Yesterday, after years of hard work and a great amount of
adverb of time ↑
effort, we finally reached the South Pole and beat our British
↑ first person expanded noun phrase ↗
competitors. What a fantastic adventure this has been!
↖ expanded noun phrase ↑ exclamation

Before our trip, one of my crew members had a wonderful idea
↑ adverbial of time ↑ opinion
to improve our sleds. What was his great idea? He made the
↑ rhetorical question
sleds lighter to make it easier to pull them! The man is a genius,
↑ opinion
and he definitely helped us save time and energy.
↑ coordinating conjunction

chronological order ↓ subordinating conjunction
Our trip began in early January when we changed our plans
past tense ↑ ↑ adverbial of time ↑ word ending in -ed
at the last minute to head to the South Pole rather than the
North Pole. We altered our plans because another team of
↑ word ending in -ed fact ↗
explorers had already reached the North Pole.
↖ fact

Eventually, we arrived at the Bay of Whales in Antarctica on
14th January. Quickly, we set up camp and started preparing
word ending in -ed ↑
everything we were going to need if we were
subordinating conjunction ↑
going to be successful on our mission.

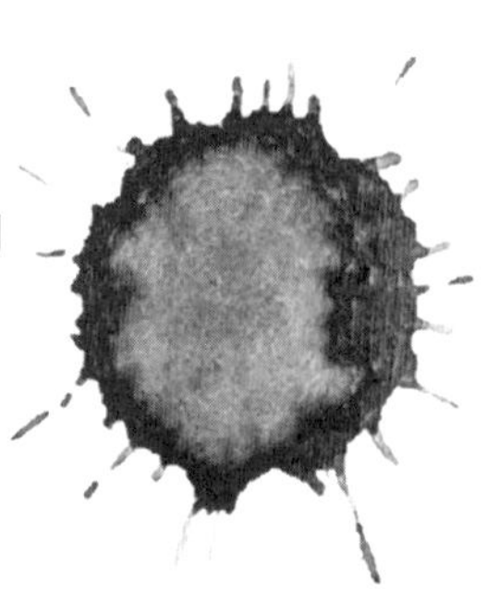

Grammarsaurus KS1© Mitch Hudson and Anna Richards 2021

As soon as we were fully prepared, it was time to set off. It was now mid-April. Our aim was to reach the South Pole within
↑ first person
ten months and we were sure we would be able to achieve our goal. We wanted to arrive by October, but we agreed that
↑ coordinating conjunction
it might take longer if the weather turned bad. This is exactly what happened on our first attempt. Was this enough to put
rhetorical question ↗
us off our task? Of course not!
↖ rhetorical question

When the weather had improved, we set out again and made
↑ subordinating conjunction
↓ expanded noun phrase
fact ↘
a second attempt with a much smaller team. This time, we
↙ fact
travelled with five people, four sleds and fifty-two dogs. To start
↑ comma for list
with, we travelled quickly. But soon we had to slow down when we reached deep, dangerous crevasses.
↑ comma for list

↓ adverb of time
Finally, after we'd completed nearly two months of difficult
↑ subordinating conjunction
travelling, we reached the South Pole on 14th December. I was
↑ word ending in -ed
close to tears because I was so pleased to have made it!
↑ subordinating conjunction
exclamation mark ↑
I planted the Norwegian flag in the ground, so I could prove
↑ adverbial of place
↑ coordinating conjunction
↓ apostrophe for omission
we'd been there. It was all worth it for we had beaten
↓ expanded noun phrase
the British team's attempt.
↑ apostrophe for possession

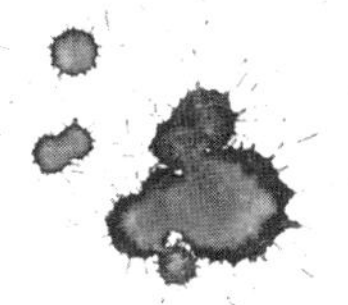

↓ sign off
Roald Amundsen

Recounts: newspaper articles

The purpose of a newspaper article is to inform and entertain the reader by providing news on current affairs.

Tips for teaching children to write newspaper articles

- Engage children in the topic of newspapers and reporting by setting up a scene to 'investigate'. For example, an alien invasion or a break-in. You could ask adults in school to be eyewitnesses and allow the children to interview them. This can make it much easier for the children to write a report.

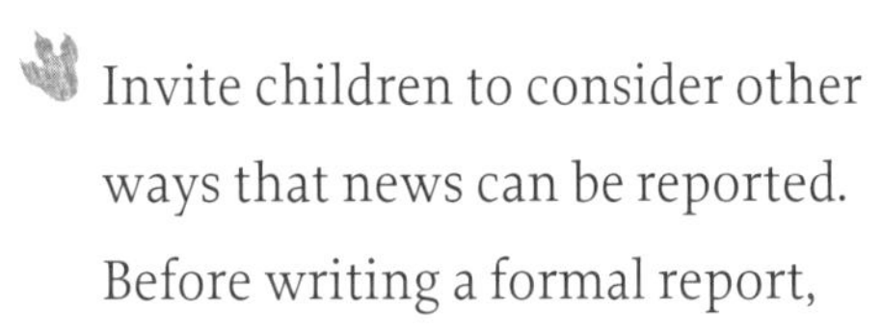

- Invite children to consider other ways that news can be reported. Before writing a formal report, could the children create their own version of a news TV show such as *Newsround*? Record the children and play the recording back to them so that they can critique how informative their show was.

Grammarsaurus KS1© Mitch Hudson and Anna Richards 2021

Choose an image or headline and ask children to write an orientation (the opening paragraph of a newspaper report) in groups. Remind them to use the five 'w's: who, what, where, when and why. You could make a table like the one below and make picture cards with options to go in each box to make this exercise even more accessible.

When	Who/what (subject)	Where	What happened?
Last night,	Bearwood House	on Linden Road	was broken into.
Last week,	a bank	in Plymouth	was raided.

When children write newspaper reports, they can run the risk of writing a narrative story instead. Remind children to avoid figurative or overly-descriptive language so that their reports remain factual.

Newspaper reports are a good chance to revise speech punctuation. Whilst inverted commas are not required to meet the expected or greater depth standard in Year 2, it is great to introduce basic speech punctuation before the children go into Year 3. You could use the acronym SCAPS to teach children how to correctly punctuate direct speech and the order in which punctuation marks should be used.

- **S: Speech marks**
- **C: Capital letter**
- **A: Actual words spoken**
- **P: Punctuation**
- **S: Speech marks**

There is no Year 1-level text for this chapter.
The chapter contains two Year 2 texts.

Year 2 overview

Use this overview and the checklist alongside the Year 2 model texts (pages 84 – 91).

Specific features for this text type

Feature	Example
A headline to attract the reader's interest	*Goldilocks Breaks In!*
A byline – the author of the article	
An orientation paragraph – a summary of the main points of the article	*Last night, a house in Lower Bearwood was broken into and trashed by an intruder.*
Body of the article – more detail about how the story unfolded	
Facts and statements	*The building was seven metres tall.*
Pictures and captions	
Quotations – extra detail and opinion	
Reorientation – a final paragraph saying where the story might go next	*Police are still investigating...*
Third person	
Past tense (mostly)	

The following lists should be used as a tool to help teachers plan where to cover explicit grammar, punctuation and spelling objectives from the National Curriculum Programmes of Study.

Grammar

Feature	Example
Subordinating conjunctions – expand upon independent clauses with 'when' and 'if'	*When the police arrived...*
Coordinating conjunctions – link ideas with 'but', 'so' or 'and'	*The officers looked for fingerprints, so they could find out...*
Adverbs / adverbials of place – say where events took place	*In Lower Bearwood*
Adverbs / adverbials of time – say when events took place	*Last night...* *In the early hours of the morning...*
Expanded noun phrases – add detail using 'from' and 'of'	*calls from upset neighbours* *the investigating officer*
Questions	*Who could have done it?*

Grammarsaurus KS1© Mitch Hudson and Anna Richards 2021

Punctuation

• Commas – for lists	*the living room, bedrooms and kitchen*
• Apostrophes for possession (GDS)	*the bear's house*

Spelling

- Year 2 'common exception words' from the National Curriculum: see page 9 of this book for a list of these. These common exception words are highlighted in the Year 2 model texts.
- Words ending in -ment, -ful, -less and -ly. *enjoyment, hurtful, hopeless, badly*

Checklist

Use this checklist with the Year 2 model texts. See page 7 for more information.

Headline	
Byline	
Orientation	
Body	
Facts and statements	
Pictures and captions	
Quotations	
Reorientation	
Third person	
Past tense	
Grammar: Subordinating conjunctions	
Grammar: Coordinating conjunctions	
Grammar: Adverbs / adverbials of place	
Grammar: Adverbs / adverbials of time	
Grammar: Expanded noun phrases	
Grammar: Questions	
Punctuation: Commas	
Punctuation: Apostrophes for possession (GDS)	
Spelling: Year 2 common exception words	
Spelling: Words ending in -ment, -ful, -less and -ly	

LONDON'S BURNING!

Monday 3rd September 1666

By James McAdams

In the early hours of yesterday morning, a huge, blazing fire started in a baker's shop in Pudding Lane. But how did this happen? Someone forgot to put out the oven fires, so the house caught alight and then spread, causing devastation across much of London!

The fire started in a house belonging to a baker called Mr Thomas Farynor. When he was questioned later, he said, "I checked all five fire hearths in my house and I was sure that the fires were out!" His family were woken up early in the morning by a huge fire in the ground floor of their house, so they were not able to use the stairs and they had to climb through an upstairs window to escape!

By mid-morning, many families had tried to escape because the fire was spreading so quickly. People ran to escape the blaze, but this was almost impossible.

Some people said that the fire was so large that it could be seen from a quarter of a mile

Grammarsaurus KS1© Mitch Hudson and Anna Richards 2021

Year 2 model text 1

↓ **The fire spreading through the city**

away. By the afternoon, more than three hundred houses had already been destroyed.

By last night, the great fire had spread over half a mile. King Charles II ordered the Mayor of London to pull down some of the houses because he thought it would stop the spread of the fire. This didn't work. The houses were so tightly packed together that it was impossible to pull down enough houses to stop the fire. It seems that stopping it is an incredibly difficult task!

The mayor has now ordered that people do not bring any carts near the fire after many locals tried to do this to collect their goods. Also, eight fire posts will be created with thirty soldiers at each one to try and stop the damage spreading any further.

Year 2 model text 1: annotated

Dark grey highlights = common exception words

↓ headline

LONDON'S BURNING!

Monday 3rd September 1666

By James McAdams
↑ byline

orientation
In the early hours of yesterday morning, a huge, blazing fire started in a baker's shop in Pudding Lane. But how did this happen? Someone forgot to put out the oven fires, so the house caught alight and then spread, causing devastation across much of London!

(adverbial of time; adverbial of time; comma for list; apostrophe for possession; adverbial of place; adverbial of place; question; question; third person; coordinating conjunction)

↓ body
The fire started in a house belonging to a baker called Mr Thomas Farynor. When he was questioned later, he said,

(fact and statement; fact and statement; fact and statement; subordinating conjunction)

↓↑ body
"I checked all five fire hearths in my house and I was sure that the fires were out!" His family were woken up early in the morning by a huge fire in the ground floor of their house, so they were not able to use the stairs and they had to climb through an upstairs window to escape!

(quotation; quotation; quotation; expanded noun phrase; expanded noun phrase; coordinating conjunction)

↓↑ body
By mid-morning, many families had tried to escape because the fire was spreading so quickly. People ran to escape the blaze, but this was almost impossible.

(adverbial of time; word ending in -ly; coordinating conjunction)

↓↑ body
Some people said that the fire was so large that it could be seen from a quarter of a mile

↓ picture and caption

↓ **The fire spreading through the city**

↓↑ body

away. By the afternoon, more than three hundred houses had already been destroyed.

↓↑ body

enough houses to stop the fire. It seems that stopping it is an incredibly difficult task!

↑ expanded noun phrase

↓↑ body

By last night, the great fire had spread over half a mile. King Charles II ordered the Mayor of London to pull down some of the houses because he thought it would stop the spread of the fire. This didn't work. The houses were so tightly packed together that it was impossible to pull down

↑ adverbial of time — fact ↗ — ↖ fact — ↑ subordinating conjunction — ↑ past tense — ↑ word ending in -ly

reorientation ↓

The mayor has now ordered that people do not bring any carts near the fire after many locals tried to do this to collect their goods. Also, eight fire posts will be created with thirty soldiers at each one to try and stop the damage spreading any further.

adverbial of place ↗ — ↖ adverbial of place

Gunpowder, Treason and Capture!

6th November 1605

By Henry Carter

Early yesterday morning, a shameless man, who goes by the name of Guy Fawkes, was arrested in the basement of the Houses of Parliament. He was charged with high treason for trying to kill King James I!

↖ **Guy Fawkes**

After being alerted by Lord Monteagle that something awful was going to happen to James I, the King's guards thankfully were able to find Guy Fawkes and some of his fellow conspirators under the Houses of Parliament. These ruthless men had decided to use gunpowder to blow up the building exactly where the King and Parliament would be positioned. Their spiteful plan was to cause an enormous explosion, but luckily, this plan did not work!

When the guards searched the basement, they found thirty-six barrels of gunpowder. This was twenty-five times more than they actually needed! But why did these men want to kill the King, how was their plan foiled, and what will their punishment be?

It is understood that Guy Fawkes and his group of plotters were Catholics who were frustrated about the way they were being treated in Protestant England. They wanted to improve their treatment and to make England a Catholic country again. Lord Monteagle had been warned by letter to avoid attending Parliament on the 5th of November, so he also told other people not to attend.

After he was arrested, Fawkes tried to get away with the crime by lying and giving the guards a false name – John Johnson! When he was asked why he had tried to complete such a hateful crime, Fawkes said, "A desperate disease requires a dangerous remedy!"

The King has declared that Fawkes will be hanged, drawn and quartered for his crimes in the new year. Around the country, people will light bonfires because they want to honour the King still being alive!

↓ **The Houses of Parliament**

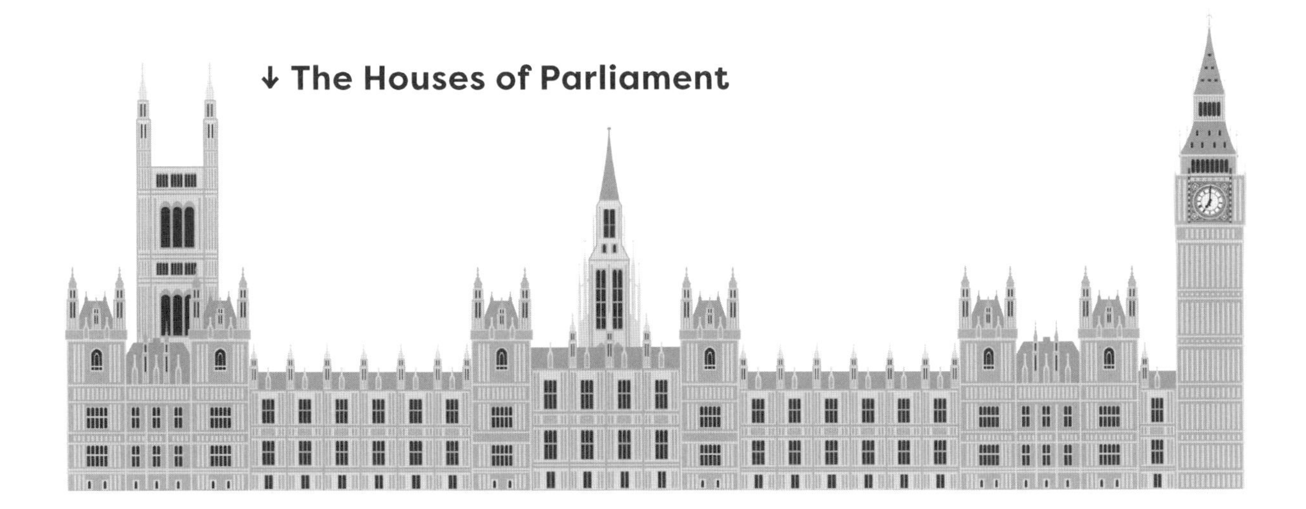

Year 2 model text 2: annotated

Dark grey highlights = common exception words

↓ headline

Gunpowder, Treason and Capture!

6th November 1605

By Henry Carter
↑ byline

orientation

Early yesterday morning, a
↑ adverbial of time
shameless man, who goes by the
↑ word ending in -less
name of Guy Fawkes, was arrested
in the basement of the Houses
adverbial of place ↗
of Parliament. He was charged
↖ adverbial of place
with high treason for trying to
kill King James I!

↖ **Guy Fawkes**
↑ pictures and captions

body

After being alerted by Lord
Monteagle that something awful
was going to happen to James I,
↓ word ending in -ly
the King's guards thankfully were
↑ apostrophe for possession
able to find Guy Fawkes and
some of his fellow conspirators
under the Houses of Parliament.
These ruthless men had decided
↑ word ending in -less
to use gunpowder to blow up
the building exactly where the
King and Parliament would be
positioned. Their spiteful plan was
↑ word ending in -ful
to cause an enormous explosion,
↑ expanded noun phrase
but luckily, this plan did not work!
↑ coordinating conjunction

↓↑ body

When the guards searched
↑ adverbial of time and third person
the basement, they found
fact and statement ↗
thirty-six barrels of gunpowder.
↖ and statement
This was twenty-five times more
↖ fact and statement
than they actually needed!
↖ fact and statement
But why did these men want
↑ questions

Grammarsaurus KS1© Mitch Hudson and Anna Richards 2021

↓↑ body ↓ comma for list

to kill the King, how was their
↑ questions

plan foiled, and what will their
↑ questions

punishment be?
↑ word ending in -ment

↓↑ body

It is understood that Guy Fawkes and his group of plotters were Catholics who were frustrated about the way they were being treated in Protestant England. They wanted to improve their treatment and to make England a Catholic country again. Lord Monteagle had been warned by letter to avoid attending Parliament on the 5th of November, so he also told other people not to attend.

coordinating conjunction ↑ (so)

↓↑ body

After he was arrested, Fawkes tried to get away with the crime by lying and giving the guards a false name – John Johnson! When he was asked why he had tried to complete such a hateful crime, Fawkes said, "A desperate disease requires a dangerous remedy!"

↑ past tense (tried)
↑ word ending in -ful (hateful)
↑ quotation
↑ quotation

reorientation

The King has declared that Fawkes will be hanged, drawn and quartered for his crimes in the new year. Around the country, people will light bonfires because they want to honour the King still being alive!

comma for list ↑
subordinating conjunction ↑ (because)

↓ **The Houses of Parliament**

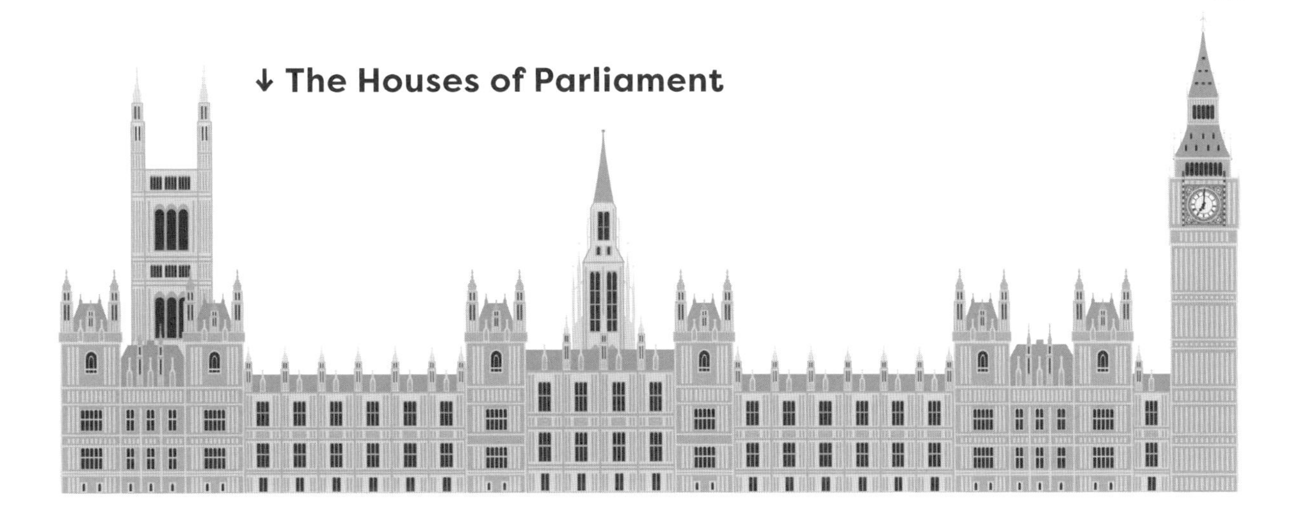

Persuasive texts

The purpose of a persuasive text is to encourage the reader to buy a product or buy into an idea.

Tips for teaching children to write persuasive texts

- Immerse children in the world of persuasive writing before they write their own persuasive texts. Encourage children to look at adverts in magazines or brochures and watch adverts on TV so that they can identify how persuasive language is used.

- Children could write persuasive texts in the form of a poster or even create their own radio or TV adverts. Ask the children to consider how they might need to change their text, depending on whether they're writing for TV or radio (where the listener won't be able to see the product).

- If the children are writing a persuasive text about a real-life event, consider how their writing could be adapted to other non-fiction text types. The children could write a non-chronological report about the event or a diary entry from the perspective of someone who went to the event.

Grammarsaurus KS1© Mitch Hudson and Anna Richards 2021

- If children are writing about a product, invite the class to identify its unique selling point (USP). Write the USP on the board for children to see (make it the centre of a brainstorm). Annotate the USP with different language features children could use to explain the USP. For example, would they want to use an expert opinion to give the claims about the product credibility?

- Encourage children to use a thesaurus and language clines to learn new persuasive vocabulary. A language cline is a scale of language that goes from one extreme to another, for example:

    - **euphoric**
    - **overjoyed**
    - **cheerful**
    - **glad**
    - **content**

- Create triples! Persuasive writing has so many examples of the rule of three. Invite children to watch or read examples of speeches and adverts, for example, toy adverts or trailers for new children's films. Then, use this to create lists of three as a class. You could use images as a stimulus for this. If the children are writing about a product, invite them to think about three problems the product would solve. Then, for each problem, children can write the solution the product provides. You could encourage the children to make a big deal about these problems using rhetorical questions, in order to persuade the reader that this product is the answer to all their issues!

- Teach comparatives and superlatives when children are writing persuasive texts. Encourage the children to think about when it is appropriate to use comparatives and superlatives.

Year 1 overview

Use this overview and the checklist alongside the Year 1 model text (pages 96 – 97).

Specific features for this text type

• Deals and bargains	***...and get 20% off.***
• Direct address to the reader (can include flattery)	***You deserve the best.***
• Facts and statistics	***There's only one magic carpet in the whole world.***
• Opinion (can be an expert opinion)	***The princess said it was the best.***
• Rhetorical questions	***Do you want to fly through the skies?***
• Emotive / exaggerated language	***It will change your life!***
• Triples / the rule of three	***beautiful, magical and cheap***

The following lists should be used as a tool to help teachers plan where to cover explicit grammar, punctuation and spelling objectives from the National Curriculum Programmes of Study.

Grammar

• Personal pronouns – speak directly to the reader with the second person 'you'	***You deserve to experience a magic carpet!***
• Expanded noun phrases – for exaggeration	***the most amazing sights*** ***a fun magic carpet ride***
• Coordinating conjunctions – link ideas with 'and'	***Book a ride and tell your friends!***

Punctuation

• Question marks	***Are you looking for a magical carpet?***
• Exclamation marks	***What a good offer!***

Grammarsaurus KS1© Mitch Hudson and Anna Richards 2021

Spelling

- Year 1 'common exception words' from the National Curriculum: see page 9 of this book for a list of these. These common exception words are highlighted in the Year 1 model texts.

Checklist

Use this checklist with the Year 1 model text. See page 7 for more information.

Deals and bargains	
Direct address (can include flattery)	
Facts and statistics	
Opinion (can be an expert opinion)	
Rhetorical questions	
Emotive / exaggerated language	
Triples / the rule of three	
Grammar: Personal pronouns	
Grammar: Expanded noun phrases	
Grammar: Coordinating conjunctions	
Punctuation: Question marks	
Punctuation: Exclamation marks	
Spelling: Year 1 common exception words	

Year 1 model text

Are you looking for some magic beans?

We have the perfect beans for you!

You will love the beans as they will grant your wishes, bring you gold and make you happy.

You need the best beans and Jack's beans are the very best.

These beans are cheaper here than anywhere else. They are better than any other beans in town. In fact, 95% of buyers would buy them again!

Buy our amazing beans today and all of your friends will be jealous!

Special offer
Buy three beans and get one more for free!

Grammarsaurus KS1© Mitch Hudson and Anna Richards 2021

Year 1 model text: annotated

Dark grey highlights = common exception words

Are you looking for some magic beans?

↑ rhetorical question — question mark ↑

We have the perfect beans for you!

↑ expanded noun phrase — exclamation mark ↑

You will love the beans as they will grant your wishes, bring

↑ second person pronoun — ↑ rule of three ⟶

you gold and make you happy.

↑ rule of three ⟶

You need the best beans and Jack's beans are the very best.

↑ direct address — ↑ coordinating conjunction — ↑ opinion

These beans are cheaper here than anywhere else. They are

better than any other beans in town. In fact, 95% of buyers

↑ statistics ⟶

would buy them again!

↑ statistics ⟶

Buy our amazing beans today and

coordinating conjunction ↑

all of your friends will be jealous!

↑ emotive language ⟶ ↖ exclamation mark

Special offer

deals and bargains

Buy three beans and get one more for free!

Year 2 overview

Use this overview and the checklist alongside the Year 2 model texts (pages 100 – 107).

Specific features for this text type

Feature	Example
Deals and bargains	*...and get a free pair of shoes.*
Direct address to the reader (can include flattery)	*You would look perfect in this!*
Alliteration and assonance	*a brilliant bargain*
Facts and statistics	*Three-quarters of our customers agree that...*
Opinion (can be an expert opinion)	*Fashion experts agree that...*
Repetition	*Buy it. Wear it. Love it.*
Rhetorical questions	*Are you looking for an ideal gown for the ball?*
Emotive / exaggerated language	*This will be the best purchase you ever make.*
Triples / the rule of three	*elegant, regal and beautiful*

The following lists should be used as a tool to help teachers plan where to cover explicit grammar, punctuation and spelling objectives from the National Curriculum Programmes of Study.

Grammar

Feature	Example
Personal pronouns – speak directly to the reader with the second-person 'you'	*You need a wonderful outfit!*
Coordinating conjunctions – link ideas with 'and'	*...and don't forget to get yours today.*
Subordinating conjunctions – expand upon independent clauses with 'because'	*...because all of your friends will be jealous.*
Expanded noun phrases – for exaggeration	*a one-of-a-kind opportunity*
Commands – instruct the reader	*Grab a bargain now!*

Punctuation

Feature	Example
Question marks	*Are you searching for a new look?*
Exclamation marks	*It is the most wonderful place on Earth!*
Apostrophes for possession (GDS)	*the gown's fabric*

Grammarsaurus KS1© Mitch Hudson and Anna Richards 2021

Spelling

- Year 2 'common exception words' from the National Curriculum: see page 9 of this book for a list of these. These common exception words are highlighted in the Year 2 model texts.

• Words ending in -ing	*looking, searching, wishing, amazing, hoping*
• Words ending in -est	*greatest, happiest, biggest, tallest*
• Words ending in -ful	*colourful, delightful, powerful, wonderful*

Checklist

Use this checklist with the Year 2 model texts. See page 7 for more information.

Deals and bargains	
Direct address (can include flattery)	
Alliteration and assonance	
Facts and statistics	
Opinion (can be an expert opinion)	
Repetition	
Rhetorical questions	
Emotive / exaggerated language	
Triples / the rule of three	
Grammar: Personal pronouns	
Grammar: Coordinating conjunctions	
Grammar: Subordinating conjunctions	
Grammar: Expanded noun phrases	
Grammar: Commands	
Punctuation: Question marks	
Punctuation: Exclamation marks	
Punctuation: Apostrophes for possession (GDS)	
Spelling: Year 2 common exception words	
Spelling: Words ending in -ing	
Spelling: Words ending in -est	
Spelling: Words ending in -ful	

Grammarsaurus KS1© Mitch Hudson and Anna Richards 2021

T-Rex in town

March – May at Lodingford Town Hall

The truly terrifying dinosaur exhibition is finally here!

Visit now to avoid disappointment.

You deserve to visit the best attraction in town!

Are you transfixed by triceratops, dotty about diplodocuses or spellbound by stegosauruses? Are you amazed by dinosaurs, but don't know where to go?

Then you should come to our show because it is the best place to see not only the most realistic dinosaurs, but also the greatest range of these weird and wonderful creatures in England. Even Dr. Dave, the Dino Expert, agrees that this is the best place to see these amazing beasts, and he is the country's leading palaeontologist.

Tickets

Single entry: £4.50

Family pass: £15

You won't find tickets cheaper than ours in the whole country, but, if you do, we will match the price so you don't waste your money.

Nine out of ten visitors to our incredible attraction say they will return to see the dinosaurs again soon!

These dangerous dinosaurs are sure to scare and amaze both adults and children. Visit us now and see for yourself!

Grammarsaurus KS1© Mitch Hudson and Anna Richards 2021

Year 2 model text 1: annotated

Dark grey highlights = common exception words

T-Rex in town

↑ alliteration

March – May at Lodingford Town Hall

↓ alliteration →

The truly terrifying dinosaur exhibition is finally here!

↖ word ending in -ing — exclamation mark ↑

Visit now to avoid disappointment.

↑ command →

You deserve to visit the best attraction in town!

↑ flattery — ↑ expanded noun phrase

↓ personal pronoun

Are you transfixed by triceratops, dotty about diplodocuses or

↑ rule of three and alliteration → ↓ rhetorical question

spellbound by stegosauruses? Are you amazed by dinosaurs,

↑ rule of three and alliteration →

but don't know where to go?

question mark ↑

Grammarsaurus KS1© Mitch Hudson and Anna Richards 2021

Then you should come to our show because it is the best
↑ subordinating conjunction

place to see not only the most realistic dinosaurs, but also

the greatest range of these weird and wonderful creatures
↑ word ending in -est ↑ word ending in -ful

in England. Even Dr. Dave, the Dino Expert, agrees that this
↑ expert opinion

is the best place to see these amazing beasts, and he is
↑ word ending in -ing ↑ coordinating conjunction

the country's leading palaeontologist.
↑ apostrophe for possession

Tickets

Single entry: £4.50

Family pass: £15

You won't find tickets cheaper than ours in the whole country,
↑ exaggeration

but, if you do, we will match the price so you don't waste your
↑ deals and bargains

money.

Nine out of ten visitors to our incredible attraction say they
↑ statistic

will return to see the dinosaurs again soon!

These dangerous dinosaurs are sure to scare and amaze
↑ alliteration

both adults and children. Visit us now and see for yourself!
↑ repetition of 'visit us now'

Grammarsaurus KS1© Mitch Hudson and Anna Richards 2021

Year 2 model text 2

Adopt a wild animal!

Do you adore animals? Are you fearful for the safety of our most precious wild animals? Would you like to improve your own awareness of the Earth's most beautiful creatures?

If so, join today and adopt an animal for as little as £3.50 per month. It is sure to be one of the greatest things you'll do this year because this is the gift that will keep on giving.

If you are an animal lover, then this could be the perfect present for you! Help end illegal hunting, stop habitats being destroyed and provide training for the people trying to protect these beautiful creatures. All you need to do is pay £3.50 every month and the rest is up to us. Our experts will then use your money to make sure these helpless animals are protected.

Grammarsaurus KS1© Mitch Hudson and Anna Richards 2021

When you sign up, you'll be asked to choose an animal. Once your payment is taken, we will send you your information pack so you can find out more about your wonderful new adoptee.

- **We have lost 90% of our African elephants in the last century.**
- **There are less than 3,900 tigers left in the wild today.**
- **There are only 1,860 giant pandas remaining in the wild today.**

These numbers are worryingly low, but your money could help change this!

Make a change. Be the change. See the change. These defenceless animals' lives are in your hands. Without your support, wild animals like these are at risk of extinction. Act fast!

Join today and get a free cuddly toy with your starter pack!

Year 2 model text 2: annotated

Dark grey highlights = common exception words

Adopt a wild animal!

Do you adore animals?
↑ rhetorical question and direct address →
Are you fearful for the
↑ word ending in -ful
safety of our most

precious wild animals?
question mark ↑
Would you like to improve

your own awareness

of the Earth's most

beautiful creatures?

↓ command →
If so, join today and adopt an animal for as little as £3.50 per
↑ coordinating conjunction
month. It is sure to be one of the greatest things you'll do this
↑ opinion ↑ word ending in -est
year because this is the gift that will keep on giving.
↑ subordinating conjunction

alliteration ↗
If you are an animal lover, then this could be the perfect
↖ alliteration ↓ rule of three →
present for you! Help end illegal hunting, stop habitats
↓ rule of three →
being destroyed and provide training for the people trying to
↑ word ending in -ing ↑ word ending in -ing
↓ rule of three →
protect these beautiful creatures. All you need to do is pay
↑ word ending in -ful
£3.50 every month and the rest is up to us. Our experts will
↑ coordinating conjunction
then use your money to make sure these helpless animals
↑ emotive language
are protected.

Grammarsaurus KS1© Mitch Hudson and Anna Richards 2021

When you sign up, you'll be asked to choose an animal.
↑ second person pronoun

Once your payment is taken, we will send you your information pack so you can find out more about your wonderful new adoptee.

deal ↗ ↖ deal
expanded noun phrase ↑
↑ word ending in -ful

facts and statistics

- **We have lost 90% of our African elephants in the last century.**
- **There are less than 3,900 tigers left in the wild today.**
- **There are only 1,860 giant pandas remaining in the wild today.**

↑ word ending in -ing

These numbers are worryingly low, but your money could help change this!
↑ exclamation mark

↓ rule of three / repetition of 'change' →

Make a change. Be the change. See the change.

These defenceless animals' lives are in your hands.
↑ apostrophe for possession

Without your support, wild animals like these are at risk of extinction. Act fast!

Join today and get a free cuddly toy with your starter pack!
↑ deal

Glossary of terms

Term	Meaning	Example
active voice	When a sentence is in the active voice, the subject is doing the action.	*Holly opened the door.*
adjective	A word that describes a noun.	*tiny, big, generous*
adverb	A word that describes and qualifies a verb, adjective or another adverb.	*quickly, soon*
adverbial	A group of words that is used to indicate time, place, manner or frequency.	*After school, I attended football club.*
antonym	A word opposite in meaning to another word.	*bad / good* *beautiful / ugly*
apostrophe	For omission: to replace letters which have been omitted. For possession: to show something belongs to someone or something.	*should not / shouldn't* *Jithu's jumper*
brackets	A pair of marks used for parenthesis.	*Queen Elizabeth II (Britain's longest-reigning monarch) was crowned in 1953.*
bullet points	Used for lists.	• *sugar* • *butter* • *flour*
capital letter	Used at the start of a sentence or for a proper noun.	*My cousin lives in Scotland.*
clause	A part of a sentence that contains a subject and a verb.	*I went to my friend's house.*
cohesion	Using words and phrases to link paragraphs or sentences to help guide a reader.	*It was beginning to rain. However, the children could still go outside as they had umbrellas.*

Grammarsaurus KS1© Mitch Hudson and Anna Richards 2021

Term	Meaning	Example
colon	Used to detail the previous clause by answering or explaining the idea within it. Colons can be used at the start of a list if there is an independent clause before the punctuation.	*The verdict had been reached: guilty!* *I packed only essential items in my bag: a toothbrush, a hairbrush and some pyjamas.*
comma	Used to separate items in a list and for a parenthesis.	*I packed my teddy bear, pyjamas and a toothbrush.* *The Eiffel Tower, which is located in Paris, is 324 m high.*
command	A sentence (beginning with an imperative verb) which tells someone to do something. It can end with an exclamation mark or a full stop.	*Put your toys away.* *Stop what you're doing!*
coordinating conjunction	A word used to join independent clauses in a sentence.	*for, and, nor, but, or, yet, so*
dashes	These marks can be used like brackets or to introduce a new clause.	*I put your present in the post – it will arrive in three days.*
determiner	A word that introduces a noun and can give more detail.	*a, the, some, any, my, your*
direct speech	Writing the actual words of a speaker using inverted commas (speech marks).	*"Where are you?" Jason asked.*
ellipsis	Used to show that one or more words have been missed out or that a sentence is not finished.	*But who knew what horrors lurked behind the door...*
exclamation	A group of words or sentence which shows surprise, emotion or pain. It does not have to include 'what' or 'how' unless you want it to be an exclamation sentence (see below).	*I did it!*
exclamation mark	A mark at the end of an exclamation or exclamation sentence.	*It was raining again!*
exclamation sentence	A sentence which shows surprise, emotion or pain. It ends with an exclamation mark and must start with either 'what' or 'how' and include a verb.	*What a wonderful day it is!*
expanded noun phrase	A group of words that serves the same function as a noun in a clause.	*a scary giant* *a witch on a broom*

Term	Meaning	Example
hyphen	Used to connect two or more words.	*dagger-like, twenty-one*
inverted commas	Used at the start and end of direct speech (and are also known as speech marks).	*"Let's go!" said mum.*
modal verb	Used to express ideas such as possibility, intention, obligation and necessity.	*can, could, should, might, shall, ought to*
noun	A person, place or thing.	*Queen Elizabeth, London, crown*
parenthesis	A word or phrase inserted as an explanation or afterthought (can be punctuated with brackets, dashes or commas).	*Julia – my auntie – gave me a brilliant birthday present.*
passive voice	When a sentence is in the passive voice, the subject of the sentence is acted on by the verb.	*The door was opened by Aisha.*
past / present / future tense	Past: something happened / has happened. Present: something happens / is happening. Future: something will happen / is going to happen.	*I was* *I am* *I will be / I'm going to be*
plural	More than one thing.	*two men* *two dogs* *two babies*
possessive pronoun	A pronoun showing possession.	*mine, yours, his, hers, ours, theirs*
prefix	Letters added to the start of a word.	*disagree, unhappy*
preposition	A word which shows a noun's relationship to another word in the sentence. It often shows where or when something is.	*under, over, before, beside*
pronoun	A word used to replace a noun.	*I, she, they, his, them*
punctuation	Marks we use in writing.	*. / , / ? / !*
question	Something you ask. It ends with a question mark.	*What is your name?*
question mark	A mark to show the end of a question.	*How will the story end?*
relative clause	Used to explain or describe something that has just been mentioned.	*The dog, which was black and white, chased after the ball.*
relative pronoun	A pronoun that introduces a relative clause.	*when, who, which, where, that, whom*

Grammarsaurus KS1© Mitch Hudson and Anna Richards 2021

Term	Meaning	Example
semi-colon	A punctuation mark used to separate longer, detailed items in a list or to link related clauses.	*She noticed three things: there was dirt on the wall; the door was broken, hanging off one hinge; and the smell was disgusting.* *It was starting to snow; the children grabbed their scarves and gloves.*
sentence	A group of words with a verb that makes complete sense.	*The man had a dog.*
singular	One thing.	*one man* *one dog* *one baby*
statement	A sentence which states something. It ends with a full stop.	*I like animals.* *I feel happy.*
subjunctive form/mood	Used to express doubt, wishes or a recommendation.	*The police have recommended that all drivers stay clear of the city centre.*
subordinate clause	A clause that doesn't make sense on its own. It begins with a subordinating conjunction.	*I ate my dinner quickly because I was hungry.*
subordinating conjunction	A word at the start of a subordinate clause.	*because, when, if, unless*
suffix	Letters added to the end of a root word.	*jumping, beautiful*
synonym	A word that means exactly or nearly the same as another word.	*smile / grin* *black / ebony*
verb	An action.	*run, walk, jump*

Further teaching tips and acronyms

Over the years, we have used a range of acronyms and teaching ideas which have helped us when teaching non-fiction writing. Check out some of our favourites below.

Coordinating conjunctions: FANBOYS

You can use the acronym FANBOYS to teach the different coordinating conjunctions.

I am going shopping and I am buying food for dinner.

F	for
A	and
N	nor
B	but
O	or
Y	yet
S	so

Formal / informal

This table will help children identify when they might use a formal or informal tone of voice. Remember that sometimes children might need to use formal and informal language, for example, in an advert they might change from a formal to an informal tone to address the reader directly.

Formal	Informal
A letter to a gas company	A message to a friend
A job application	An email to your cousin
A police report	A postcard
A letter of complaint	A note to your parents

Formal	Informal
Avoid contractions ***will not***	Use contractions ***won't***
Avoid slang / colloquial language ***It is raining heavily.***	Use slang / colloquial language ***It's raining cats and dogs.***
Use formal equivalence ***Stop eavesdropping.***	Use phrasal verbs ***Stop listening in.***
Avoid question tags ***That is right.***	Use question tags ***That's right, isn't it?***

Subordinating conjunctions: A WHITE BUS

You can use the acronym **A WHITE BUS** to teach children the different subordinating conjunctions.

We couldn't go to the swimming pool because it was shut for repairs.

A	WH	I	T	E	B	U	S
although after as	when whenever whatever whether whereas which	if in order that in case	though till that	even if even though	because before	until unless	since

Grammarsaurus KS1© Mitch Hudson and Anna Richards 2021